Mysterious Places

Other books in the Fact or Fiction? series:

Mysterious Places

Fact or Fiction?

Tom Head, *Book Editor*

Daniel Leone, *President*

Bonnie Szumski, *Publisher*

Scott Barbour, *Managing Editor*

OPPOSING
VIEWPOINTS®
SERIES

GREENHAVEN
PRESS®

THOMSON

——————✳——————™

GALE

San Diego • Detroit • New York • San Francisco • Cleveland
New Haven, Conn. • Waterville, Maine • London • Munich

THOMSON
★ ™
GALE

Acknowledgments

Tom Head extends special thanks to project editor Kyla Stinnett, managing editor Scott Barbour, and production editor Carolyn Cronin. Charlie Brenner of the Jackson/Hinds Library System, Sherry Stroup of Kessler-Hancock Information Services, and Shane Hunt of 4ResearchSolutions.com all played an instrumental role in helping to locate hard-to-find research materials. As always, Tom Head would also like to thank his family for their love and support.

FEB 14 '05

LIBRARY OF CONGRESS CATALOGING-IN-PUBLICATION DATA
Mysterious places / Tom Head, book editor.
p. cm. — (Fact or fiction)
Includes bibliographical references and index.
ISBN 0-7377-1643-6 (alk. paper) — ISBN 0-7377-1644-4 (pbk. : alk. paper)
1. Parapsychology. 2. Curiosities and wonders. I. Head, Tom. II. Fact or fiction (Greenhaven Press)
BF1031.M96 2004
001.94—dc21   2003044899

Printed in the United States of America

Contents

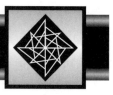

Foreword

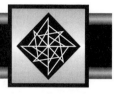

"There are more things in heaven and earth, Horatio, than are dreamt of in your philosophy."
—William Shakespeare, *Hamlet*

"Extraordinary claims require extraordinary evidence."
—Carl Sagan, *The Demon-Haunted World*

Almost every one of us has experienced something that we thought seemed mysterious and unexplainable. For example, have you ever known that someone was going to call you just before the phone rang? Or perhaps you have had a dream about something that later came true. Some people think these occurrences are signs of the paranormal. Others explain them as merely coincidence.

As the examples above show, mysteries of the paranormal ("beyond the normal") are common. For example, most towns have at least one place where inhabitants believe ghosts live. People report seeing strange lights in the sky that they believe are the spaceships of visitors from other planets. And scientists have been working for decades to discover the truth about sightings of mysterious creatures like Bigfoot and the Loch Ness monster.

There are also mysteries of magic and miracles. The two often share a connection. Many forms of magical belief are tied to religious belief. For example, many of the rituals and beliefs of the voodoo religion are viewed by outsiders as magical practices. These include such things as the alleged Haitian voodoo practice of turning people into zombies (the walking dead).

There are mysteries of history—events and places that have been recorded in history but that we still have questions about today. For example, was the great King Arthur a real king or merely a legend? How, exactly, were the pyramids built? Historians continue to seek the answers to these questions.

Then, of course, there are mysteries of science. One such mystery is how humanity began. Although most scientists agree that it was through the long, slow process of evolution, not all scientists agree that indisputable proof has been found.

Subjects like these are fascinating, in part because we do not know the whole truth about them. They are mysteries. And they are controversial—people hold very strong and opposing views about them.

How we go about sifting through information on such topics is the subject of every book in the Greenhaven Press series Fact or Fiction? Each anthology includes articles that present the main ideas favoring and challenging a given topic. The editor collects such material from a variety of sources, including scientific research, eyewitness accounts, and government reports. In addition, a final chapter gives readers tools to analyze the articles they read. With these tools, readers can sift through the information presented in the articles by applying the methods of hypothetical reasoning. Examining these topics in this way adds a unique aspect to the Fact or Fiction? series. Hypothetical reasoning can be applied to any topic to allow a reader to become more analytical about the material he or she encounters. While such reasoning may not solve the mystery of who is right or who is wrong, it can help the reader separate valid from invalid evidence relating to all topics and can be especially helpful in analyzing material where people disagree.

Introduction

During the early morning hours of June 21, 2003, nearly thirty thousand people gathered around an intricately arranged circle of large rocks located in the southern English city of Wiltshire. As 4:46 approached, their excitement grew. "This is not a rave," said a twenty-nine-year-old man named Andrew. "It is better than a rave . . . it is about the stones."[1] The revelers had come to observe the summer solstice, the longest day of the year in the Northern Hemisphere and a holy day in many religious traditions. As the sun rose above Stonehenge's massive Heel Stone, the crowd beat drums and erupted into cheers.

There was more to the event than a beautiful sunrise. Stonehenge, a ring of stone circles, was constructed in such a way that the sun rises directly above the Heel Stone every summer solstice. It has done so for over three thousand years. By visiting the site on summer solstice, the British celebrants are participating in an ancient tradition on a mysterious site that predates recorded European history.

The Story of the Stones

Although the origins and purpose of Stonehenge remain mysterious, some basic facts about the monument are no longer subjects of serious dispute. The monument consists of a series of large stones carefully arranged in four layers inside a circular trench three hundred feet in diameter. Carbon dating suggests that the monument was built in phases between 3000 B.C. and 1500 B.C. from a mix of common sandstones and less common Welsh bluestones.

On nearly all other matters pertaining to Stonehenge, archaeologists frequently disagree. One subject of controversy is who built Stonehenge. It has traditionally been believed that Stonehenge was built by an ancient English culture, but recent evidence has suggested that some of the builders may have been Swiss. Archaeologists discovered the grave of an extremely wealthy figure (dubbed "the king of Stonehenge") buried with treasures in the Stonehenge area during the period of its construction (about 2300 B.C.). Recent chemical tests on his teeth indicate that he was almost certainly an immigrant from the Alpine region of Europe who had originally lived in or near Switzerland.

Another baffling issue is Stonehenge's purported astronomical properties. Archaeologists have long suspected that Stonehenge's axis accurately points to the sunrise during the summer and winter solstices. In 1965 astronomer Gerald S. Hawkins published a comprehensive study (*Stonehenge Decoded*) of Stonehenge's astronomical alignments, claiming that stones on its axis correspond to the spring and fall equinoxes and can be used to predict eclipses. Although some disagree with Hawkins's hypothesis, many still regard it as credible.

As Hawkins himself acknowledged, however, deciphering the astronomical properties of Stonehenge does not yield further knowledge of its purpose. Although most scholars agree that Stonehenge functioned as a center for religious rituals, it most likely had one or more specific purposes that are not yet fully understood. Some have suggested that it is a burial site, based on the fact that graves have been found nearby. It has also been widely suggested that Stonehenge may have functioned as a site for executions or human sacrifice, owing to the presence of an ancient headless skeleton in a nearby grave and the etymology of the word *Stonehenge* (which comes from *Stonehanges*, or "Stone Gallows"). And a new theory has been brought forth by obstetrician Anthony Perks, who argues that Stonehenge may have been intended as a fertility symbol (owing to its resemblance to female genitalia).

Archaeologists have been debating the origins and intended purpose of Stonehenge for centuries. Many new theories and a great deal of scientific data pertaining to Stonehenge have emerged within the past decade, destroying past theories and leaving open the faint possibility that Stonehenge, as mysterious as it is, may one day be explained by traditional archaeology. Many argue, however, that Stonehenge's riddle will never be solved by traditional archaeology alone.

Alternative Theories

Many alternative archaeologists (those who hold unorthodox views about ancient culture) argue that the world's mysterious places are connected in some way. In his 1925 book *The Old Straight Track,* English businessman and expert geographer Alfred Watkins argued that Stonehenge and other sacred and cultural sites in England were lined up along prehistoric trading routes that he described as "leys" and which are more commonly described today as ley lines. During the 1950s and 1960s, belief in ley lines spread—and with it, the belief that ley lines have supernatural significance, representing conduits of spiritual energy.

Belief in ley lines is popular in England, where the theory hinges largely on the mysterious nature of Stonehenge and other stone circles that can be found throughout the English landscape. Stonehenge, it is often believed, is the work of an ancient and spiritually advanced civilization created by druids (ancient priests of pre-Christian Britain). Some have hypothesized that these druids were followers of Tout, a chief god in the ancient Celtic pantheon. What makes Tout rare among most ancient deities is that he is both a ruler god and a messenger god. (In most systems of world mythology, the messenger god is given relatively little power over other gods in the pantheon.) This suggests a culture that placed social importance and spiritual emphasis on roads and the act of traveling them. If the ley lines are roads of spiritual energy, then they could be earthly manifestations of the power attributed to Tout.

Some alternative archaeologists attempt to locate these roads by searching for spiritual energy through a process known as dowsing, traditionally used to find water. The dowser finds whatever he or she is looking for by holding out a somewhat flexible but reasonably firm object—such as a light tree branch or a bent coat hanger—and following its vibrations. Many dowsers believe that these vibrations are the spiritual energy of ley lines. For those who believe that these ley lines have spiritual properties, Stonehenge is a nerve center of ancient supernatural energy. "I call this place the battery," said enthusiastic English tour guide Nick Kendrick in a 1998 interview. "Can you feel all the energy coming out of it?"[2]

The Missing Empire

Whereas some look to England's ley lines as evidence of Stonehenge's unusual properties, others believe that these properties have less to do with its geography than with the highly advanced people who built it. For millennia, many have believed that an ancient globe-spanning culture once ruled Earth, building monuments and spreading knowledge on every continent. Although some consider the idea ridiculous today, it was popularized by one of the most revered rational philosophers in the Western tradition: the ancient Greek philosopher Plato (428–328 B.C.). In his dialogue

Timaeus (360 B.C.), Plato quotes his hero, the philosopher Socrates, as stating that:

> Histories tell of a mighty power which unprovoked made an expedition against the whole of Europe and Asia. . . . This power came forth out of the Atlantic Ocean. . . . But afterwards there occurred violent earthquakes and floods; and in a single day and night of misfortune . . . the island of Atlantis . . . disappeared in the depths of the sea.[3]

Many alternative archaeologists believe that some of the world's mysterious places were built by this ancient race of seafaring people living on a doomed continent. It has been written that these people came from an advanced civilization that once dominated the world. Some agree with Plato's description and argue that the lost continent was located in the Atlantic Ocean, but others believe that a similar continent known as Mu, or Lemuria, once existed in the Pacific Ocean.

In explaining Stonehenge as a relic of this lost culture, alternative archaeologists cite the existence of equally ambitious monuments found on other continents. "Stonehenge and its mysteries do not stand in isolation," writes author Graham Hancock. "Megaliths on an even larger scale were used in ancient Peru and Bolivia . . . [and] equally huge blocks were used to build the anonymous 'valley' and 'mortuary' temples of Giza in Egypt and the temple of the Sphinx."[4] The giant *moai* statues on the remote Easter Island, for example, are frequently cited as proof that there was once an ancient globe-spanning culture.

Unconventional theories are appealing in part because there is no single conventional explanation with which to replace them. Archaeologists do not agree about Stonehenge's original purpose, the meaning it might have held for its builders, and even who, precisely, those builders were.

The Nazca Lines

Thousands of miles away from Stonehenge, carved in the parched desert plains of Peru, lies a mystery that seems even more elusive. In the barren *pampa colorada* (red plains) of southern Peru, archaeologists have discovered more than one thousand massive carved line drawings, many visible only from the air. The Nazca lines (named after the Nazca civilization of pre-Incan Peru) cover over four hundred square feet of desolate, long-abandoned land—a region that, according to science writer Jack McClintock, "receives at most one inch of rain a year, less than the Gobi and Arabian deserts and Death Valley."[5]

Peruvian archaeologist Toribio Mejía Xesspe (1896–1983) first discovered the line carvings in 1927. Impressed with the intricate carvings, Xesspe—who did not have access to aerial photography at the time, and therefore could not get a bird's-eye view of them, believed that they signified walking paths used for religious processions. It was American archaeologist Paul Kosok (1896–1959) who first gave serious attention to a most unusual property of the Nazca lines: Many of them were so large that they could only be seen from the air. Describing the lines as "the world's largest astronomy book," Kosok argued that some of the Nazca lines correspond flawlessly to certain astronomical events. One line, for example, is said to line up with the sunset at every winter solstice.

Although Kosok laid the groundwork for an astronomical interpretation of the Nazca lines, the site did not receive widespread attention until it caught the eye of German adventurer Maria Reiche (1903–1998). In addition to introducing the Nazca lines to the mainstream American and European media, Reiche took Kosok's central hypothesis—that the Nazca lines corresponded to astronomical events—and developed it into a theory that became the dominant explanation of Nazca for decades to come and remains the most well-known theory today. She also led a movement to protect the lines from the damage caused by tourism.

In recent decades, archaeologists have proposed many diverse explanations for the Nazca lines. Some argue that their primary function was to serve as water routes, a necessary function given the area's climate. Others believe—as Xesspe did—that the lines were meant to serve in ceremonial processions. Whatever function the Nazca lines might have served, it is abundantly clear that they were created with great effort and determination, which suggests a serious goal of some kind. "The pampa isn't just a conglomeration of dysfunctional doodles on a gigantic sketchpad," writes archaeologist Anthony F. Aveni. "There is order, a pattern and a system, behind the geoglyphs."[6]

A Cosmic Welcome Mat

As traditional archaeologists continue to search for an explanation for the Nazca lines based on the culture and traditions of ancient Peru, some writers believe that the carvings may have been inspired by a civilization from another world. Swiss author Erich von Däniken expressed this theory in his best seller *Chariots of the Gods?* (1968), in which he argues that many world monuments may have been influenced by visitors from other worlds (a perspective that has become known as the alien astronaut theory). Because some of the Nazca drawings are fully visible only from the skies, von Däniken regards them as potentially strong evidence of extraterrestrial influence:

> Seen from the air, the clear-cut impression that the 37-mile-long plain of Nazca made on *me* was that of an airfield! . . . What is wrong with the idea that the lines were laid out to say to the "gods": "Land here! Everything has been prepared as you ordered"? The builders of the geometrical figures may

have had no idea what they were doing. But perhaps they knew perfectly well what the "gods" needed in order to land.[7]

In addition to von Däniken's hypothesis, other controversial theories have been proposed to explain the unusual aerial properties of the Nazca lines. Some say that ancient Nazca priests traveled outside of their bodies through mysticism, allowing them to survey the landscape from above and report instructions to their followers below. Others have suggested that, as in the case of Stonehenge, the Nazca lines could be the relics of an ancient worldwide civilization. Like that of Stonehenge, the original purpose of the Nazca lines remains unknown to archaeologists.

Pilgrimage

The solstice revelers went to Stonehenge for a variety of reasons. Many, no doubt, just enjoyed the music and party atmosphere. Others may have seen it as a wonderful opportunity to get stone drunk and sing in public. Yet many went because they felt that there was a tangible spiritual energy to the experience—something that connects the monument to a society ancient beyond their comprehension, to a people who perhaps knew a great many things that have since been forgotten. Solstices are as ancient as the planet, and the idea that a largely unknown society celebrated those solstices gives many a sense of permanence and spiritual awakening.

Many people make religious pilgrimages to sites sacred to their own traditions, sites that connect them, in some way, with a reality that they believe can never be restricted by humankind's conventional understanding of time and space. There is a connection between the solemn medieval travelers who made pilgrimages to the ancient Christian site of Canterbury and the UFO aficionados who visit the purported UFO crash site at Roswell, New Mexico, to buy bumper stickers and alien masks. This connection is the search for a meaning and reality larger than themselves. To others, ancient monuments are mysterious only in a practical sense: They are puzzles waiting to be solved.

The articles in this book address both mysterious places from the ancient past and mysterious places that have recently seized people's interest. By studying the mysterious places described in this book, the reader may gain a better understanding of how human beings think about the unknown.

Notes

1. Quoted in Jason Hopps and Pete Harrison, "Stonehenge Draws Solstice Revelers," *Reuters*, June 21, 2003.

2. Quoted in Helen Chappell, "Roll Up for the Mystery Tour," *Times*, October 10, 1998, p. 29.

3. Plato, *Timaeus*, trans. Benjamin Jowett. New York: Charles Scribner's and Sons, 1871. Available online through Project Gutenberg. www.gutenberg.org.

4. Graham Hancock, *Heaven's Mirror: Quest for the Lost Civilization*. New York: Crown, 1998.

5. Jack McClintock, "The Nasca Lines Solution," *Discover*, December 2000, p. 74.

6. Anthony F. Aveni, *Between the Lines: The Mystery of the Giant Ground Drawings of Ancient Nasca, Peru*. Austin: University of Texas Press, 2000, p. 234.

7. Erich von Däniken, *Chariots of the Gods?* Trans. Michael Heron. New York: Putnam, 1970, p. 17.

Chapter 1

Fact or Fiction?

Evidence That Ancient Monuments Have Mysterious Origins

The Great Pyramid Is Part of a Network of Spiritual Energy Sites

Art Bell and Brad Steiger

The awesome and enduring design of the Great Pyramid has led many thinkers to suspect that conventional accounts for its origins may not be accurate. Some have proposed that the Great Pyramid might have been built by a civilization far more advanced than that of dynastic Egypt—perhaps even an extraterrestrial civilization, or telekinetic builders from the lost continent of Atlantis.

In this excerpt from their book *The Source* (1999), former late-night radio talk show host Art Bell and paranormal scholar Brad Steiger argue that the Great Pyramid was built by ancient and mysterious master builders as part of a globe-spanning network of spiritual energy sites.

Art Bell and Brad Steiger, *The Source: Journey Through the Unexplained.* New Orleans: Paper Chase Press, 1999. Copyright © 1999 by Art Bell and Brad Steiger. Reproduced by permission of the publisher.

There it stands before you, the Great Pyramid of Giza—the stuff of which legends, dreams, and alternate states of reality are fashioned. At last you are really here, standing before it, beholding its awesome presence as if it is an archetype from the unconscious that has suddenly manifested in the ancient desert sands of Egypt. Inspired lines of poetry, the tributes of emperors and kings, the awestruck journals of early explorers, and the cinematic efforts of a dozen epics have all attempted to pay adequate tribute to this most magnificent of structures.

Visualizing the Great Pyramid

If you allow your psyche to open fully to the experience, you will no doubt feel at one with a thousand or more vibrations of those who have entered these stone portals before you.

And yes! It is really you going inside the Great Pyramid! You are actually doing it yourself—not vicariously allowing Charlton Heston, Harrison Ford, Cecil B. DeMille, or Steven Spielberg to do it for you.

But you do not simply walk into the King's Chamber. You climb—crawl really—on a steep incline through a very small tunnel slanting upward for at least a hundred yards. Then you emerge into a larger chamber in which, you are relieved to note, you can once again stand upright. But the climb isn't over. You have even steeper steps to surmount until you at last enter the King's Chamber.

If you expect a movie-set tomb when you enter the chamber, you will be disappointed. All the glorious golden artifacts and the mummies were removed a long time ago. All that remains is this vast bare room with a large, open sarcophagus at one end.

In the Sarcophagus

[Coauthor] Art [Bell] had quite an amazing experience when he lay down within the sarcophagus. [According to Bell]

> I don't know what got into me, but after a long climb to the King's Chamber, I took one look at the giant sarcophagus and I knew that I wanted to do what most people couldn't. What would it be like to be inside an ancient Egyptian coffin, to feel the presence of thousands of years—to lie down with kings in the middle of the oldest, largest structure in the world? I wasn't prepared for the experience.
>
> First of all, you have to understand that the Great Pyramid at Giza is not just any structure. We'd already been to Greece and seen the Parthenon, one of the pinnacles of human achievement in architecture and design. But to put it simply, Giza is from another world entirely. In fact, how and why it was constructed is one of the world's great puzzles.

Mathematical Properties

Mathematically, the Giza Pyramid is laid out based on geographical information that no human being could have possibly had at that time. For example, according to [physicist and author] John Zajac, it is placed in the direct center of Earth's landmass, both in longitude and latitude. This would require intimate knowledge of Africa, Europe, and the new worlds. Including the entire planet, the average height of land above sea level (as can be measured only by modern satellite) is 5,449 inches—the exact height of the Great Pyramid.

But there's something even more fantastic. Zajac tells us that, mathematically, the construction of the pyramid's inner tunnels and chambers duplicates major religious events in human history, including the Jewish Exodus and the birth and death of Jesus.

Was the Great Pyramid based on spiritual knowledge? Could the necessary information to construct the pyramid have been supplied by extraterrestrials? Who knows? We only know that it is truly the most amazing, so-called "human structure," bigger than thirty Empire State Buildings. And there I am—deep inside it, right in the King's Chamber, stepping into the giant stone sarcophagus of the pharaohs.

As I lay down in the coffin what I experienced was something I will never forget. It was not the echo of my voice as I spoke from the sarcophagus, but the vibrations that I felt when I spoke. It was as if my voice became the Voice of the Ages, as if somehow an ancient coffin made of cold stone had come to life. I could feel what "Egyptians" from almost 5,000 years ago must have experienced as they placed the giant coffin in the room—which is at the center of the giant pyramid.

I smelled the damp, musty odor of the coffin; and I thought of the hugeness of the stone monument in which I was encapsulated. It was truly hard to imagine the centuries of darkness endured by that room. As I lay there, I felt very small and very human—and very awake. Talk about a feeling of self-awareness.

The Message of the Great Pyramid

John Zajac once gave [radio program] *Dreamland* listeners a guided tour of the Great Pyramid after which he concluded that:

Clearly, whoever built the Pyramid had access to information beyond that which earthlings possessed at that time— at least earthlings as we know them. Now, one can argue that we were visited by scientifically advanced beings from outer space who [sic] taught us their technology. . . . If so, these advanced beings had the paramount goal of leaving behind a message that would endure for eons.

. . . The message would have to be universal yet simple, survive the centuries, and be understood by all the Earth's inhabitants despite language and cultural differences. . . . So far the message indicates that whoever built the pyramid knew the Earth well: the length of the year, the radius of curvature, the standard measurement techniques, the average height of the continents, and the center of the landmass. They were able to construct something that we still cannot construct today, and they were able to tie all these things together in this single structure.

[Coauthor] Brad [Steiger] described an eerie phenomenon . . . that occurred when he visited the King's Chamber:

Since we were standing in what is probably the single most mystical pilgrimage point for metaphysicians on the entire planet, I felt compelled to lead a very brief creative visualization of a possible past life that our souls might have experienced in ancient Egypt.

Afterward, when I turned to touch the right forefinger of the person next to me, a strange, high-pitched sound filled the King's Chamber. All around me I noticed members of the group uncomfortably turning their heads and scrunching their shoulders toward their ears.

How would I describe the sound? If you saw *2001: A Space Odyssey*, you couldn't forget the piercing sound the monolith made when it was uncovered on the Moon and beamed its signal toward Jupiter. You may have noticed a similar sound in *E.T. the Extraterrestrial*, when E.T. touches his right forefinger to Elliot's right forefinger.

Vibrations of the Pyramid

Always the researcher as well as the participant, I methodically checked each of the half-dozen tape recorders in the chamber. I put my ear to the single dim electrical bulb that provided the only source of illumination in the chamber. None of the camera batteries or recorders were emitting anything other than their normal soft clicks and buzzes. The loud, piercing sound was not coming from anywhere in particular. It was coming from all around us.

Later, we discussed the manifestation back in our hotel. Some of the members of our tour group believed that the sound that we had heard had been directed toward us as a means of attuning our level of awareness more completely to the vibrations necessary for contact with higher intelligences, multidimensional beings of Love and Light. It seemed to many to be a convincing sign of confirmation that each of us had heard the same sound at the same time in a place where no such sound should have been.

Sadly, the experience had proved too intense for one of the members of our group, and it seemed as though she had literally disappeared from our midst in the King's Chamber after the sound had manifested. Even hours after we had exited the Great Pyramid, there was no trace of her. No one saw her leave the King's Chamber and we were all baffled as to what could have happened. Thankfully, the woman had been found later wandering the streets of Cairo in a disoriented state of mind and had been taken to the home of a kind Egyptian family until she was able to contact the proper authorities and be returned to our group.

The Source

There is no question that such powerful places as the Great Pyramid have strange and mysterious effects upon those pilgrims who visit these sacred and significant sites. And there is no telling what incredible discoveries will be made in the next few years that will link our past to our future in ways not yet dreamed of by the average man or woman.

Somehow these great monuments and ancient city sites are connected with the mysteries of what elements comprise the true nature of Time and who we as a species truly are. And for those of us who seek the Source of paranormal phenomena, we are driven to explore the sacred sites and holy places of the Earth for clues to the origin of our deepest and most profound enigmas.

Mysterious phenomena that run the gamut from the appearance of UFOs to the manifestations of spirit beings have been widely reported in many places: the Sphinx, the Great Pyramid of Giza, and Luxor in Egypt; Masada, Qumran, and Jerusalem in Israel; the ancient Nabatean city of Petra in Jordan; Machu Picchu, Ollantaytambo, and Sacsahuaman in Peru; Tiahuanaco in Bolivia; and the red rock vortexes of Sedona, Arizona.

Why are these areas so revered? Did the ancients sense that certain physical locations contained somehow within themselves a power that encouraged the realization of prayers, meditation, and altered states of consciousness? Perhaps there are electromagnetic frequencies at work here.

Or other energies not yet identified by our sciences that literally open a doorway between dimensions.

Interestingly, if one were to conduct an excavation beneath the great cathedrals, churches, and synagogues of Europe, one would find the even older remains of a place of worship cherished by ancient practitioners of the Old Religion. If one were to conduct similar digs beneath the great cathedrals, churches, and synagogues of North and South America, one would be likely to find evidence that the grounds on which they were constructed were considered sacred and holy by the native people of the region.

Perhaps the ruins of great cities of lost civilizations around the planet are considered sacred because of memories within the collective unconscious of *Homo sapiens* that cherish the presence of the mysterious master builders from elsewhere who constructed such magnificent tributes to a dimly remembered past.

The British Stone Circles Are a Network of Spiritual Energy Centers

Christopher Castle

In 1925 rural English businessman Alfred Watkins proposed that ancient English sites, if examined on a map, line up along what he called ley lines—or "fairy roads"—that he regarded as prehistoric trading routes. More recent thinkers have argued that these ley lines represent focal points of spiritual energy, meeting places between material Earth and a more subtle transcendent reality. Geomancers—those who study the alternative science of spiritual place—often identify spiritual sites through a somewhat mystical process commonly described as "dowsing," in which human beings visit a site and attempt to tap into its spiritual properties.

Christopher Castle, "Nature's Teaching: The Art and Science of Geomancy," *ReVision*, vol. 21, Spring 1999, p. 39. Copyright © 1999 by Heldref Publications. Reproduced by permission.

Christopher Castle, an English artist and geomancer who has studied ley lines extensively and visited a number of stone circle sites, believes that Stonehenge and other British stone circles have spiritual properties. In this article, he argues that the spiritual phenomena represented by British stone circles such as Stonehenge can help us connect to the universe on a deeper, transcendent level.

Geomancy (from the Greek for earth divination) has come to mean the study and practice of placement of buildings and other structures in the landscape. Feng shui is a complex and highly developed form of geomancy. However, not only in China but in cultures throughout the world people have evolved geomantic practices appropriate and specific to their own locales. In all cases the influence of land forms, water flow, climate, and other features of the environment are considered and wrapped into a ritual context. Before McDonald's reached Siberia or Dallas flickered on TVs in Chad, a rich diversity of building traditions linked to life ritual could be encountered everywhere. Like feng shui, local geomantic practices evolved from the experience of people, living in close contact with the Earth. There are still traces of those traditions to be seen in many places. As an example of an early geomancy we shall explore a seemingly distant world that even today sheds light on geomancy as a universal practice.

The study of the prehistoric, megalithic cultures in Europe has surprising relevance to current concerns over our culture's disconnection from our locale. All along the western and northern seaboard of Europe there are traces of a late Stone Age culture dated by archaeology to the fifth to the third millennia before the current era (B.C.E.). There are few settlement sites, indicating a nomadic or seminomadic life, but many thousands of huge stones, called megaliths, stand arranged in circles and other formations. They present an enigma that is not clarified by the simplistic archaeological notion of a ceremonial site.

Stonehenge, in southern England, is certainly the best known of the circles, unique in its familiar trilithon (three stone) construction of massive standing slabs supporting lintel stones. Less known is the existence of more than 900 other stone circles in Britain and Ireland. Collectively these sites, when viewed together with the many vast earthworks, cairns, chambered mounds, dolmens, and individual stones that are common in the landscape of the British Isles, represent a vast outpouring of expression of a largely forgotten culture. A careful exploration of their design and layout, their location in relation to geographical context, their interrelation with other sites, and the underlying geometrical prototypes and a survey of horizon features surrounding them uncover modes of intent in their construction not immediately evident to the casual observer or indeed to the orthodox archaeologist working with a nonholistic approach. Add to that the consideration of myth and story that often surround these sites and a rich geomantic tradition unfolds.

Geomancy and the Modern World

In the 1950s, 60s, and 70s Alexander Thom, a professor of engineering at Oxford University, made meticulous surveys of hundreds of stone circles (Thom 1967). He showed not only that stone circles are built on arcs drawn from carefully laid out Pythagorean triangles (long before Pythagoras's day), but that they incorporate a standardized unit of measure, which he called the megalithic yard. Further, he showed that the profiles of the stones themselves when viewed in conjunction with distant features on the horizon indicated directions for extreme rising and setting positions of the sun, the moon, and several major stars. Those marvelous astronomical, metrical, and geometrical aspects, taken together with mythic elements that often survive in local folk traditions, hold clues to a complete cosmology of the earth that can serve us today as a model of ecological dynamics. A mode of "sacred engineering" emerges as the Neolithic form of geomancy, the profoundly integrative practices of which may be applicable in any cultural context and especially in our own.

Our contemporary culture has created a fragmented environment that too often lacks the symbols that provide integration or a means of attuning to the specifics of place. Contemporary art might easily be enlisted to collaborate with the new sciences in bringing about a renaissance of bioregional organic building. A holistic approach to building and design that includes careful use of local materials, local craft knowledge, an understanding of the power of form and symbol to affect our sense of place, together with the lessons learned from the global perspective on geomantic traditions will renew our sense of integration with the places we live and our feeling for community. Such holism would steer perception toward a renewed sensibility for nature and away from the often utilitarian track of current construction methods that only enhance our separation from natural rhythm. Inclusion of the mystical essence of the animistic paradigm of the ancient sites need not be viewed, as it is by hardheaded science, as some fanciful romanticized nostalgia for things past, but as a way of reinvigorating creative design. . . .

Viewed as a form of geomancy, prehistoric landscape engineering using materials of earth and stone in symbolic ways can be seen as an activity that contributed crucially to the continued well-being of the population. Such is the vast extent of these works that they represent the major under-taking of Neolithic culture. Today our science, art, religion, politics, law, and community health are treated as separate fields presided over by specialists. The Neolithic sites and their artifacts demonstrate a holistic geomantic perception that combines all of these dimensions. Chi is focused through multiple means that are simultaneously applied in the design of the sites. The symbolic form (of, say, a circle) is merely the outer shell of a multi-layered complex of in-tent that is written into them.

Because I am an artist my research has been free of the need to stay within the archaeological strictures of counting and measuring. My responsibility has been to extract mean-ing from those fascinating places with the full application of intuition, supported by careful scholarship that includes archaeological research combined with contemporary eco-logical and psychological understanding. Working with the premise that a direct perceptual approach uncovers more subtle information that is embedded in the material of these ancient structures than would be available to the of-ten fragmenting approach of archaeology, I have examined many of the sites to discover what I can of their cultural context and even of the cosmology that underlies them. . . .

A Visit to Boscawen-Un

On midsummer's eve I walk along the sheltered track that leads to Boscawen-Un stone circle in Cornwall, in south-west England. I have studied both the orthodox archaeo-logical papers that describe the sites and John Michell's (1974) analysis of the many standing stones of this region that points to an elaborate pattern of lines linking them. But all of that is back in my library in London. Now I wish to apply my own experience to Boscawen-Un, one of the key sites in Michell's scheme.

As I approach I begin to feel the playfulness of the local spirits, the piskies. Gusts of wind tug at my hair; brambles lash my legs; there is a twittering in the hedge; a rabbit momentarily runs ahead of me and vanishes. As the evening sun just tips the hedges and walls I pick my way through the gorse bushes and suddenly find myself at the circle. Each of the nineteen stones is only a few feet high, but at the center stands the magnificent sloping pillar I have heard about. Entering the ring I move from stone to stone touching each as I go, feeling their varied surfaces. Each seems to have a personality drawn by its unique form, mass, and texture. On the far southwesterly side I come to something quite special, a great block of quartz. Though no larger than the others, its radiance and glow draw my attention. I decide I shall come to watch tomorrow's sunrise from beside this stone.

As I contemplate the form of the circle in the changing light, I move to a place opposite the sun and sit down to watch. Quickly now the sun sinks to the horizon, casting shadows of the stones towards me. I feel a powerful realization as the stones before me line up with the solar disc. I visualize the geometry of the circle. Thom's survey shows a geometrically flattened shape. This shape is barely perceptible, but I can see that the direction of the sunset closely coincides with a line across the ring's wider axis. I feel the geometry activated for an instant as the light crosses the stones. Rapt, I visualize subtle pulsating bands spreading outward as if the stones somehow trap and amplify the event. The lost sunbeam just touches the tip of the sloping central pillar and is gone.

Windswept clouds swim low across the sky in the twilight. As the darkness takes over, the stones become vague, shadowy figures. Soon the shapes of the hedges, the nearby ridges, and the far horizon merge in a single silhouette against the final glow of the day. One by one stars flicker in the breaks between clouds as I make my way back to my camp.

I awake early. Venus is a bright morning star now, shining intermittently between the predawn clouds. Wafts of lilac light come and go in the northeast. I go to the stones. This time I am here to see if my intuition concerning the inclined center stone is accurate. Something convinces me that the angle of the central stone is not accidental. Nor was the stone, as archaeologists have mistakenly believed, ever placed vertically. With a compass I have surmised that the direction of its tilt coincides with the dawn I am about to witness—the summer solstice. I sit down in line with its slope and prop myself against my quartz block. All I can see is the pointed tip leaning away from me, dark against the growing dawn light. The clouds scud by, momentarily lighting an ethereal yet earthy scene. My mind, clear and awake now, is sharpened by the chill air and by my own anticipation.

Reflecting the Horizon

I think of the mob waiting at Stonehenge. For centuries the midsummer sun rising over the outlying Hele Stone and along the major axis of the site's geometry has drawn crowds of intrigued enthusiasts. But here at Boscawen-Un, it seems a million miles from all that. Peace prevails, no one but myself and the full complement of nature beings is here to see the spectacle. And spectacle it is! There is an occasional rustle as a soft gust filters through the bushes caressing me and the surrounding circle. Brighter and brighter beyond my stone, the very land feels animated as if being stroked by the sun, as if being coaxed into life from the womb of the night. Slowly the stones emerge from their cover of darkness, dimly at first, then as I look from stone to stone each one's character awakens. At last the wait is over. Light is burgeoning from its predawn incubation, pulsing beyond the horizon, brighter and brighter. Will it ever come? Just when I'm thinking that a cloud bank may be hiding the sun, there is a momentary flair, and yes, the disc rises brilliant from the hedges of the fields to the northeast, a tiny point growing to a momentous, roaring wave of light. And yes, the finger of the center stone at Boscawen-Un circle does very definitely point toward the place of the sunrise at the summer solstice.

The circle becomes the receptacle for the event. It reflects in microcosmic form the horizon, the dome of the sky, the completion, the totality, the circle of life. But it is not isolated, randomly placed, or in any way accidental. Everything is brought into its sphere as the sun comes up, and the lines that are spread hereabouts in the land are charged with meaning.

The circle is sacred, encompassing a circumscribed specific area of ground set aside as a sanctuary separate from the world, a complete, ideal realm. It is an embracing, expanding continuum from this world to the other. Coming to the circle with the knowledge of its mathematical, geometrical, and astronomical dimensions opens the perceptual door to a world beyond the symbolical attributes. The very structure begins to affect consciousness. A veil is lifted, and the pattern of life itself shows through.

At such times the laws of nature often seem to come unstuck, and shifts in the fundamental principles of perception are felt as dynamic changes in body and place. As I listen to nature here, becoming quiet and opening my senses to the whole spectrum of impressions, particularly those that are sensed just on the edge of vision, at the limits of audibility—those ripples of li—my body feels swept into the magnum mysterium inseparable from the place itself. Pulsing waves of time seem to press on me, a further dimension of the spirals I saw earlier. I am carried through darkness to a place of renewal. I leave Boscawen-Un this summer morning in a blithe and vital mood, my drawings only holding a vestige of the fullness I feel, the gratitude for the gift of this new understanding. I return to London feeling that something fundamental has been recast in me.

Notes

Michell, J., *The Old Stones of Lands End.* London: Garnstone Press, 1974.

Thom, A., *Megalithic Sites in Britain.* Oxford: Oxford University Press, 1967.

Thom, A., and A.S. Thom, "A Megalithic Lunar Observatory in Orkney: The Ring of Brogar and Its Cairns." *Journal for the History of Astronomy* 4:111–123, 1973.

———, "Further Work on the Brogar Lunar Observatory." *Journal for the History of Astronomy* 6:100–114, 1975.

The Origins of
the Easter Island
Statues Are
Mysterious

Graham Hancock

The mysterious, gigantic *moai* statues that dot the landscape of remote Easter Island have captured the imagination of archaeologists for centuries. While conventional explanations of the statues hold that they were built by an ancient thriving island civilization, others maintain that other factors may have been at work.

In this excerpt from his book *Heaven's Mirror* (1998), journalist and political activist Graham Hancock argues that an ancient and highly advanced lost civilization built the statues of Easter Island. As evidence, Hancock cites (among other things) traditional Easter Island folklore, the island's complex native language, and the high quality of the more ancient *moai* relative to later monuments.

Known to its inhabitants since ancient times as Te-Pito-O-Te-Henua, 'The Navel of the World', and as Mata-Ki-Te-Rani, 'Eyes Looking at Heaven', Easter Island stands at latitude 27 degrees 7 minutes south of the equator and at longitude 109 degrees 22 minutes west of the Greenwich meridian. These coordinates put it just a fraction over 147 degrees of longitude east of the great temple complex of Angkor Wat in Cambodia. Since there is no other habitable land for over 3000 kilometres in any direction in the surrounding wastes of the Pacific, this is as close as it is physically possible to get at present sea-level to the magical precessional figure of 144 degrees of longitude east of the 'Angkor meridian'. The island, moreover, is part of a massive subterranean escarpment called the East Pacific Rise, which reaches almost to the surface at several points. Twelve thousand years ago, when the great ice caps of the last glaciation were still largely unmelted, and sea-level was 100 metres lower than it is today, the Rise would have formed a chain of steep and narrow antediluvian islands, as long as the Andes mountain-range. One link in that precipitous chain would have extended more than 300 kilometers to the west of the peak later named Te-Pito-O-Te-Henua and would have reached out towards a point in the ocean located exactly 144 degrees east of Angkor. Is it possible that some sort of solar observatory or temple of the stars might have been located at this geodetic centre in remote prehistory, later to be drowned by rising sea-levels?

Such speculation is fuelled by the fact that when the American nuclear submarine *Nautilus* made her round-the-world voyage in 1958, scientists on board 'called attention to the presence of an exceedingly lofty and still unidentified underwater peak close to Easter Island'.[1] It is a fact that Professor H.W. Menard of the University of California's Institute for Marine Resources has identified 'an important fracture zone in the neighbourhood of Easter Island, a zone parallel to that of the Marquesas archipelago', together with 'an immense bank or ridge of sediment'.[2] It is also a fact, not easy to explain away as coincidence, that the oldest local traditions describe Easter Island as having once been part of a 'much larger country'.[3] These traditions contain confusing and contradictory elements but all agree that in the most distant mythical past:

> a potent supernatural being named Uoke, who came from a place called Hiva . . . travelled about the Pacific with a gigantic lever with which he pried up whole islands and tossed them into the sea where they vanished under the waves. After thus destroying many islands he came at length to Te-Pito-O-Te-Henua, then a much larger land than it is today. He began to lever up parts of it and cast them into the sea [but] the rocks of the island were too sturdy for Uoke's lever, and it was broken against them. He was unable to dispose of the last fragment, and this remained as the island we know today.[4]

Other legends of the Easter Islanders tell us more about 'Hiva', the mysterious land from which Uoke is said to have come. We learn that it was once a proud island of enormous size, but that it too suffered in the 'great cataclysm' and was 'submerged in the sea'.[5] Afterwards, a group of 300 survivors set out in two very large ocean-going canoes to sail to Te-Pito-O-Te-Henua, having magically obtained foreknowledge of the existence of the island and of how to steer a course towards it using the stars.[6] . . .

Magic and Geodesy

From the dawn of its strange history, almost up to the time of first contact with Western civilization in the eighteenth century, Easter Island was ruled by a dynasty of god-kings.

The founder of this dynasty was Hotu Matua, the leader of the fleet of two great canoes full of survivors that set sail from Hiva shortly before it sank beneath the sea.[7] Easter Island traditions tell us that this god-king, whose name means 'prolific father',[8] was accompanied by his Queen Ava-Reipua and was instructed by a certain Hua Maka, a magician, who foresaw the destruction of Hiva and made an out-of-body journey in which he located Te-Pito-O-Te-Henua as a place of refuge:

> Hua Maka had a dream in which, in spirit, he travelled over the whole of the island.[9] . . . Having looked over all the bays . . . the spirit stopped at Anakena [on the north-east coast] and cried, 'This is the place, and this is the great bay, where King Hotu Matua will come and live.'[10]

Following Hua Maka's magical vision-quest, the physical exploration of Easter Island is said to have been undertaken by seven sages—'kings' sons, all initiated men'[11]—who travelled 'from Hiva in a single canoe'.[12] It was their mission to 'open the way' for Hotu Matua and to prepare the island for settlement. . . .

Mysteries

One afternoon around the June solstice—mid-winter in the southern hemisphere—we stood on the white sand beach between the two rocky headlands of Anakena Bay. Behind us was Ahu Nau Nau, a massive stepped pyramid of hulking stone blocks culminating in a long, flat platform. Mounted on this platform, with their backs to the sea, towered seven extraordinary statues, one a torso only, one headless, one intact but bare-headed, and four wearing gigantic red stone crowns.

Some scholars have speculated that these seven 'Moai' (literally 'images'[13]) represent Easter Island's original Seven Sages, the forerunners of Hotu Matua. There can be no certainty of this, particularly since an eighth statue, squat and bizarrely formed, stands off to the side of the bay on the nearby Ahu Ature Huki. Indeed, there is no certainty about the purpose or significance of *any* of the more than 600 great statues of Easter Island.[14] They represent a nearly pristine mystery, one that has been repeatedly challenged by generations of investigators in the past three centuries but that has never been satisfactorily solved.

The mystery concerns a vanished primeval homeland— the legendary island of Hiva that was swallowed up by the sea—and the claim that a small band of people survived the cataclysm of 'Uoke's lever' and eventually settled on the rocky peak, still above the waves, that they called Te-Pito-O-Te-Henua. Are we to dismiss such traditions as pure fancy? Or could there be something to them?

The mystery concerns a people who at one time must have been accomplished seafarers—for only consummate navigators and sailors could have succeeded in bringing their vessels intact to so remote a spot as Te-Pito-O-Te-Henua.

An Unknown Culture

And the mystery also concerns a people who must already have possessed a well-developed tradition of architecture and engineering when they arrived at the 'Navel of the World'—for there is little trace of experimentation and trial-and-error in the execution of the great Moai. On the contrary, the consistent and carefully thought out artistic canon expressed in these unique works of sculpture appears to have been fully elaborated *at the very beginning* of Easter Island's remarkable statue-making phase—with the best Moai often being the earliest ones.[15]

The same goes for the massive stone platforms known as 'Ahu' on which many of the Moai stand: once again the earlier examples tend to be superior to those built later.[16]

Archaeologists believe, probably correctly, that they have got Easter Island's chronology pretty well worked out:

- The earliest accepted evidence of human settlement comes in the form of reeds—carbon-dated to A.D. 318—from a grave at the important Moai site of Ahu Tepeu.[17]
- The next evidence is charcoal, carbon-dated to A.D. 380, found in a ditch on the Poike peninsula.[18]
- The next carbon-date, A.D. 690, comes from another important Moai site, Ahu Tahai—from organic materials apparently incorporated at the time of building into the Ahu platform itself.[19]

Ahu Tahai is therefore regarded by archaeologists as 'the earliest such structure dated so far'.[20] Its Moai, on the other hand, which cannot be directly dated by radio-carbon, are thought to have been added much later. This is because what is described as Easter Island's 'earliest known classical statue'[21] stands alone just to the north of Tahai. 'Contextual' evidence, and radio-carbon tests on associated organic materials, have persuaded archaeologists to assign this 20-tonne, 5-metre-tall Moai to the twelfth century A.D.[22] Paradoxically, however, they do admit that 'the classic statue form was already well developed' by that time.[23]

Thereafter 'classical' Moai continued to be sculpted in large numbers for approximately half a millennium until the last, 4 metres tall, was erected at Hanga Kioe at around A.D. 1650.[24] Seventy-five years later, after a series of genocidal wars between the two principal ethnic groups on the island (the so called 'Long-Ears' and 'Short-Ears'), the much diminished population had its first, fateful contact with European sailing vessels. Predictably, random murders, kidnappings, systematic slave raids, and epidemics of smallpox and tuberculosis followed with such intensity that by the 1870s the population of Easter Island had been reduced to just 111 individuals. This tiny group of survivors included not a single member of the island's hereditary cast of teachers and initiated men, the Ma'ori-Ko-Hau-Rongorongo, all of whom had been abducted and carried off during a ferocious Peruvian slave raid in 1862.

Hieroglyphs

The little that is known about the Ma'ori-Ko-Hau-Rongorongo forms part of the enduring mystery of Easter Island, for the word Ma'ori in this context means 'scholar' or 'master of special knowledge'.[25]

The first of these Ma'ori masters (not to be confused with the Maori people of New Zealand) were said to have come to Easter Island with Hotu Matua himself. They were scribes, literate men. Their function was to recite the sacred words written on 67 wooden tablets that Hotu Matua had brought with him from Hiva[26] and, when the originals became rotten or worn out, to recopy the writings on to replacement tablets.

This is not a myth: 24 of the so-called 'Rongorongo tablets' have survived to this day. Their old and complete name was Ko Hau Motu Mo Rongorongo, meaning literally 'lines of script for recitation'.[27] Generally they take the form of flat wooden boards, somewhat rounded at the edges, shiny with use and age. Inscribed on these boards, in neat rows a centimetre high, are hundreds of different symbols—animals, birds, fish, and abstract shapes. Linguists point out that there are far too many of these symbols 'to suggest any sort of phonetic alphabet or syllabary'[28] and argue that they are a fully developed hieroglyphic script somewhat similar to that of ancient Egypt or of the Indus Valley civilization.[29] . . .

Oral histories collected on Easter Island make it clear that the knowledge of how to read and write this script was transmitted from generation to generation—and indeed was formally taught at a special circular schoolhouse established at

Anakena—until 1862 when the slave-raiders took away the last of the Ma'ori-Ko-Hau-Rongorongo.[30] Up until that time, when the golden thread of tradition that attached Easter Island to its past was so brutally severed, Anakena had also been the scene of an important annual festival at which 'the people were assembled to hear all the tablets read'.[31]

Some brief recitations were given to European and American investigators in the nineteenth century but the script was not deciphered. Since then several scholars have claimed to have 'cracked' the code—most recently in 1997—but none of these claims have come to anything. The truth is that today we can only guess at the contents of these sacred tablets and wonder why, for so long, they were accorded such importance by the Easter Islanders. . . .

A Single Global Culture

The mystery of Easter Island so far seems to have at least four distinct ingredients:

- the mystery of Hiva, the legendary homeland of the gods, supposedly destroyed by a flood;
- the mystery of the master mariners who first guided a fleet of refugees from Hiva to the remote shores of Te-Pito-O-Te-Henua;
- the mystery of the master architects who first conceived the great Ahu and Moai;
- the mystery of the master scribes who understood the Rongorongo inscriptions.

Such sophisticated skills are the hallmarks of an advanced civilization. To find them brought together and *focussed* on a remote island in the Pacific, apparently all at once, is extremely hard to explain in terms of the normal 'evolutionary' processes usually ascribed to human societies. An alternative that many scholars have considered, therefore, is the possibility that the Easter Islanders did *not* in fact develop these skills in splendid isolation but rather received them as an influence—as a legacy—from elsewhere.

We do not wish to dwell here on the old and tired debate about whether Easter Island was first peopled (and thus culturally influenced) from the west, i.e. from Polynesia, or from the east, i.e. from South America. Since it is obvious that the first settlers of Easter Island were master navigators and seafarers, it should also be obvious that such a people in their heyday could have travelled extensively, not only to the islands of Polynesia but also much further afield to Latin America and perhaps even beyond. We think it is for precisely these reasons that Easter Island shows clear signs of prehistoric contact with both the South American mainland and with Polynesia—the chicken and the banana, for example, could only have been introduced from Polynesia whilst the sweet potato, the bottle gourd and the totora reed could only have been introduced from South America.

At least during the early phase of Easter Island's settlement, when the people still remembered how to navigate and sail ocean-going vessels, such items are likely to have flowed quite frequently in both directions—together, we assume, with many other valuable commodities, including skills, knowledge and artistic and religious ideas. We are therefore not surprised that monolithic statues that are superficially similar to the Moai (though in far fewer numbers) have been found in the ruins of Tiahuanaco in the Andes mountains of South America more than 4000 metres above sea-level,[32] in the Marquesas islands of Polynesia,[33] and in several other locations.[34] Likewise, it does not surprise us that the Ahu of Easter Island have been compared to the *marae* platforms of Polynesia[35] and, in the case of Ahu Tahira to 'the finest Inca masonry'.[36]

We are quite sure that at least some of these comparisons are valid and that mutual influences will ultimately be proved to have been at work—though not necessarily very frequently—in the prehistoric cultures of Easter Island, South America and Polynesia. Nor is this a controversial proposition, since the majority of orthodox archaeologists would be willing to support it. What is far less certain, however, is the question of Easter Island's role in the larger scheme of things—which may have been much more than just that of a passive 'recipient' of external influences. Its efficent cadre of literate architects and sculptors, whose predecessors had found the 'Navel of the World' through extraordinary feats of astro-navigation, were clearly people of the highest determination and calibre. Until the time when evil entered their community, not long before the first contact with Europeans, they had dedicated themselves singlemindedly for hundreds of years to the creation of transcendant and awe-inspiring works of religious art.

'Those Old Workers . . .'

We are not the first to suspect that they must have been driven to do all this by an overwhelming sense of *purpose* which, if it could only be fathomed out, might offer the key to the whole labyrinthine mystery. In the words of Mrs Scoresby Routledge, an intrepid British traveller and researcher who spent a year in Easter Island between 1914 and 1915:

> the shadows of the departed builders still possess the land. Voluntarily or involuntarily the sojourner must hold commune with those old workers; for the whole air vibrates with a vast purpose and energy which has been and is no more. What was it? What was it?[37]

The possibility that we intend to pursue is that the purpose of Easter Island's high initiates may have been connected to [an] underground stream of archaic spiritual gnosis that . . . appears to have originated outside both those areas and before recorded history began. We wonder also whether the very real similarities that have been noted linking Easter Island, Tiahuanaco in South America, and various anomalous megalithic structures in the Pacific, might have as much to do with such an *ancient and indirect, third-party influence*—touching all these cultures—as with the direct contacts that did also undoubtedly occur between them.

Notes

1. [Francis] Maziere, *Mysteries of Easter Island*, [Norton, New York, 1968], 42.

2. Ibid, 42.

3. Ibid, 41.

4. [Sebastian] Englert, *Island at the Centre of the World*, [Hale, London, 1972], 45.

5. Ibid, 46–47.

6. On the navigational skills of the Polynesians, see D. Lewis, 'Voyaging Stars: Aspects of Polynesian and Micronesian Astronomy', in [*Philosophical Transactions* (published by the Royal Society), London, 1974], 133–48, 276.

7. *Mysteries of Easter Island*, 41.

8. [Alan Samagalski], *Chile and Easter Island*, [Lonely Planet Publications, Oakland, 1990], 204.

9. Cited in *Island at the Centre of the World*, 46–47.

10. Cited in *Mysteries of Easter Island*, 47.

11. Cited in ibid, 47.

12. Ibid.

13. [Thor] Heyerdahl, *Easter Island: The Mystery Solved*, [Random House, New York, 1989], 40.

14. David D. Zink, *The Ancient Stones Speak*, [Paddington Press, New York, London, 1979], 165–66.

15. *Mysteries of Easter Island*, 126–28.

16. *Encyclopaedia Britannica*, Micropaedia, Vol. 4, 333; Paul Bahn and John Flenley, *Easter Island, Earth Island*, Thames and Hudson, London, 1992, 56 ff.

17. Ibid.

18. Ibid.

19. Ibid, 56 and 148–49.

20. Ibid, 149.

21. Ibid, 149.

22. Ibid, 149.

23. Ibid.

24. Ibid.

25. *Island at the Centre of the World*, 74–75.

26. Ibid, 74.

27. Ibid.

28. Ibid, 74–76.

29. Guillaume de Hevesy, *The Easter Island and Indus Valley Scripts*, Anthropos XXXIII, 1938; Alfred Metraux, *The Proto-Indian Script and the Easter Island Tablets*, Anthropos XXXIII, 1938.

30. Heyerdahl, *Easter Island: The Mystery Solved*, 123–24.

31. Ibid, 109.

32. Ibid, 157.

33. Jo Anne Van Tilburg, *Easter Island: Archaeology, Ecology and Culture* [British Museum Press, London, 1994], 75.

34. Ibid, 74–76.

35. Ibid.

36. *Island at the Centre of the World*, 100.

37. Scoresby Routledge, cited in *Island at the Centre of the World*, 100.

Chapter 2

Fact or Fiction?

Evidence That Ancient Monuments Do Not Have Mysterious Origins

Ancient Egyptians Built the Great Pyramid

Evan Hadingham

The Great Pyramid of Giza is the largest of the Seven Wonders of the Ancient World, and the only one that still stands. With its massive size, mathematical precision, and remarkable durability, it has inspired a great number of extraterrestrial or supernatural explanations. It seems inconceivable to many that a society as technologically primitive as ancient Egypt could have constructed a monument that would be such an extremely difficult project even today. Some scientists dispute this view, arguing that there is strong evidence that the ancient Egyptians did, in fact, have the necessary knowledge and equipment to build the Great Pyramid.

In this article, archaeologist Evan Hadingham, who has written several books on ancient civilizations and their monuments, reviews contemporary scholarship in an effort to explain how the Great Pyramid could have been built us-

Evan Hadingham, "Pyramid Schemes," *The Atlantic*, vol. 270, November 1992, pp. 38–43. Copyright © 1992 by The Atlantic Monthly Company. Reproduced by permission of the author.

48

ing tools and methods that would have been available to the engineers of ancient Egypt.

On the morning of June 6, 1933, scores of laborers gathered on the Nevada rim of the Black Canyon to watch a steel bucket descend on an 800-foot cable to the dry riverbed below. The bucket contained the first load of concrete for what was to become America's greatest feat of manpower and ingenuity during the Depression: the Hoover Dam. Over the next two years, working day and night, the laborers poured enough concrete to fill two Empire State Buildings. They finally blocked the canyon with a wall some sixty stories high—"the Great Pyramid of the American Desert," as one enthusiastic reporter described it.

The pyramid comparison was apt, because the Hoover Dam was the first structure in the Western world to exceed the bulk of Egypt's 4,500-year-old Great Pyramid of Khufu (also known by his Greek name, Cheops)—a monument that, of course, had been built entirely without the dump trucks, Caterpillar tractors, jackhammers, electricity, and gasoline power available to the Hoover laborers.

The architects of the Gothic and Renaissance eras frequently built on an imposing scale, yet a half dozen of their masterworks would fit comfortably inside the Great Pyramid. (According to one estimate, it could accommodate St. Peter's, Westminster Abbey, St. Paul's, and the cathedrals of Florence and Milan.) Although the Washington Monument is about seventy feet taller than the pyramid, the pyramid is at least seventy times as heavy.

More impressive than its sheer size is the precision with which the colossal design was executed. Sir W.M. Flinders Petrie, a celebrated British archaeologist who surveyed the

Great Pyramid in 1880–1882, noted with astonishment that the errors in the layout of its foundation "could be covered by placing one's thumb on them." More recent surveys have found that the lengths of the four bases vary by no more than eight inches—an error of less than a tenth of a percent. These four base lines are also positioned so perfectly due north, south, east, and west that the greatest error in their orientation is only a twelfth of a degree.

This evidence of high precision, which has provoked many farfetched theories, including the use of prehistoric lasers and extraterrestrial architects, continues to perplex even the most level-headed researchers. Without dump trucks and jackhammers, how did the Egyptians ever manage to assemble the Great Pyramid's towering pile of 2.5 million limestone blocks? Without modern surveying instruments, how could they have controlled its shape so accurately, particularly the even 52° slope of its smooth outer casing? And how could the construction job have been accomplished in just twenty-three years, the time span allotted to Cheops' reign in the celebrated Turin papyrus? Given a ten-hour working day and a year-round building program, that works out to one block set in place every two minutes! One might doubt that after two hundred years of study such questions could ever be resolved. Yet recent years have brought to the construction debate a wave of fresh evidence and ingenious new theories. This evidence may help to dispel some of the subject's mystical trappings, and it certainly enlarges our respect for the intellectual and technical abilities of the ancient Egyptians. Much of the credit for this new research should go to Zahi Hawass, the director of the Giza plateau for the Egyptian Antiquities Organization, and Mark Lehner, a young American Egyptologist; their ambitious study of the Giza plateau has disclosed a host of previously overlooked clues. . . .

Engineering the Great Pyramid

How were the builders able to survey and control the pyramid's design so accurately? They faced a difficult architectural challenge: after establishing a level, square foundation, they needed a system to ensure that the pyramid's sides rose at a uniform angle, and that the horizontal cross-section of the monument remained perfectly square as the structure grew. If they allowed small errors to creep in, then the square would become twisted and the four sides would never meet properly at the pyramid's summit. Controlling the design would be even trickier if other structures, such as building ramps, were in the way, obscuring the pyramid's corners or sides.

How did they do it? Surprisingly, Mark Lehner was able to reconstruct exact details of the original surveying operation by studying the surface of the bedrock close to the pyramid. Here he found rows of shallow holes carved into the rock, each at least a foot or so across, running parallel to the pyramid's sides. Originally the holes probably supported wooden sighting posts; if a cord had been stretched between them, it would have provided a handy reference line for the builders as the monument grew.

While Egyptologists had known about the holes for decades, no one had bothered to plot them on paper. By doing so, Lehner was able to piece together the most likely sequence of steps involved in surveying the pyramid's base. To create a level platform for the pyramid, the builders methodically worked the bedrock down, one section after another, each time measuring and remeasuring the overall dimensions of the square base. The resulting layout was highly accurate, Lehner concluded, because of this repetitive rechecking of measurements.

But how was such measuring actually carried out? How, in particular, did the Great Pyramid's architects manage to orient the pyramid so precisely to the north, south, east, and west, and to measure lengths accurately over hundreds of feet, all without modern surveying gear? Here texts and tomb paintings offer valuable clues. In a rock-cut tomb 300 feet beneath the desert near Luxor one of the earliest known Egyptian astronomical scenes, drawn in black on the ceiling, consists of a noble procession of divinities bearing sun disks on their heads. A prominent figure holds an object about the size of a tennis-racket handle at arm's length and at eye level; this object looks like a sighting instrument—perhaps the simple wooden sighting stick known to the Egyptians as a bay. Museum specimens and later texts suggest how the bay was used to make sightings of stars. A priest would peer through a small notch carved on the top of the bay, similar to the back sight of a rifle, until he had the star in view. To help line up the star, he used other aids, such as a plumb line suspended in front of him like a rifle's front sight.

Here, in this 3,500-year-old drawing, one can also see cartoonlike images of the northern constellations: for example, the bull called Meskheti, corresponding to our Big Dipper. These northern stars were of supreme sanctity to the Egyptians, because they were the "imperishable" or "undying" stars, which never passed below the horizon into the underworld. The pyramid builders believed that the Pharaoh's soul would rise from the tomb and ascend to the northern stars to take its place among the other immortals. Cheops' architects might well, therefore, have used sightings of stars revolving around the pole to fix their accurate north-south baseline for the pyramid. The orientation could have been checked by repeated measuring of noonday shadows cast by the sun.

Two long straight lines in the drawing connect the sacred northern stars to the procession of gods below. These lines may well represent the twin cords involved in a ceremony known as "stretching of the cord," which we can again interpret with the help of other texts and images, some dating back almost to the time of Cheops. Stretching of the cord involved pulling a long loop of string taut around a pair of poles, each held by a priest; the priests then adjusted the line to match the direction of the sun or star gods in the sky. Inscriptions tell us that this act was a sacred prelude to the foundation of a temple—so sacred, indeed, that the Pharaoh himself sometimes held one of the poles.

Little imagination is required to interpret this stretching of the cord as a ritualized act of surveying; moreover, even though more rudimentary surveying gear would be hard to visualize, the procedure actually works. Experimenting in his Connecticut garden, Martin Islet, a noted pyramid-engineering researcher, found that he could extend an existing short straight line with great accuracy using poles and a long loop of string. He found that he was far less prone to error in setting out a row of stakes if he used a loop of string instead of a single strand. In fact, he easily projected a dead-straight line over more than 400 feet (and could have projected the line much farther if he had not ended up in his shrubbery).

How to Build a Pyramid

Could the experimental approach help resolve some of the bigger puzzles of pyramid engineering? The film producer Michael Barnes, shooting a documentary for the PBS NOVA series, organized the building of an eighteen-foot-high "mini-pyramid," on the employees' soccer field of the first-class hotel at the foot of the pyramid plateau.

Barnes began the project by seeking advice from Mark Lehner and two master masons, Roger Hopkins and Nick Fairplay, yet he soon discovered a reservoir of expertise among local Egyptian stonemasons. A dozen of them camped out around a kerosene stove in the desert for twenty-one days and nights; their task was to quarry 190 blocks, each weighing three or four tons. Though equipped with steel picks and cables rather than copper adzes and hemp ropes, they worked in a completely traditional manner—by first hocking a network of deep parallel channels in the soft bedrock, and then hammering in iron wedges along the base of each block to prise it free. (At the end of the operation the site exactly resembled the many ancient abandoned quarries still visible around the plateau today.)

The masons delivered the stones to the soccer field with the help of a truck and a mechanical loader. Then the low-tech experiments began, first with wooden sleds and round wooden logs as rollers. Not surprisingly, maneuvering a stone onto a sled without tipping it or smashing the wood proved extremely tricky. So did the job of keeping the sled under control once the stone was safely in place and hauling on the ropes began. Slipping rollers underneath the sled only made the problem worse, because the stone easily veered off course.

Then the laborers tried moving blocks without any sleds or rollers at all—by simply tumbling them end over end with the help of ropes lassoed around the tops of them. But the method turned out to be laborious, and how could blocks be tumbled safely and speedily up the incline of a ramp? The problem seemed more intractable than ever.

A Dispensable Ramp

Once again, local expertise proved unexpectedly effective. The secret was tafla—a local clay still regularly mined as an all-purpose mortar. Here was the ideal ramp-building material: when tafla bonded together with small stones and boulders, the resulting structure was stronger and lighter than mud brick, yet could be easily demolished with a few swings of a pick. Significantly, Lehner has identified remnants of ancient tafla ramps at several spots on the plateau, one with walls that still stand ten feet high.

Tafla was also vital in solving the problem of hauling the stones. By itself a wet tafla surface was too slippery to work on, but once wooden planks were set into it, like railway ties, the improvement was dramatic. Mark Lehner recalls the moment when they finally worked out the right technique: "We were trying to move the sled on rollers up the trackway, and had twenty men hauling away on the ropes, slipping and sweating, and we were getting nowhere. So we had a new idea—forget about the rollers and try simply sliding the sleds up the wet wood of the trackway. The masons protested furiously, 'It won't work!' but we said, 'Just give it a try!' They poured water on the wooden planks, eased the sled off the rollers, and next thing we knew it took off like a bar of soap."

Once the team had hit upon this method, hauling the stones up progressively steeper gradients proved surprisingly easy. Even the problem of turning the ramp's sharp corners was solved: stout posts were planted at each corner, and the laborers simply pivoted their ropes at right angles around the posts as they pulled around the corners. . . .

As each new level was completed, the resulting square platform would be carefully measured with strings and plumb bobs, and then compared with the previous square below. In this way Barnes and his crew could easily check critical dimensions and avoid the problem of twist. Lehner has found little socket holes drilled into many of the Great Pyramid's steps; if we suppose that these held wooden pegs that in turn supported strings, then this checking procedure was evidently the practice of the ancient builders, too.

Down to a Science

A final challenge was making sure that the casing blocks were cut to the correct angle so that the pyramid would have a smooth, uniform slope. Many armchair theorists have speculated that the Great Pyramid's angle of about 52° was the product of complex, mystical math, but the NOVA team found an elementary way to reproduce that same angle.

They measured and marked off a simple triangle on the side of each casing block—a triangle eleven units along the base by fourteen units high; such a proportion automatically gives an angle of 52°. Then the block was roughly trimmed to match the triangle.

Once a whole row of casing blocks was fitted in place, the outer surface of the pyramid was smoothed and finished; at this stage careful remeasuring and eyeballing seemed quite adequate to achieve a precise, regular structure.

With practice, the NOVA pyramid builders settled into an efficient routine. "If we'd had three months instead of three weeks to work things out," Barnes says, "we could have built our pyramid faster than you could using modern machinery."

The experiment left Mark Lehner impressed with the simplicity of the required techniques as well as the audacious scale on which the Egyptians had applied them. "It's surprising how easily it's done with a little bit of practice and common sense," he comments. "It's all very feasible. What's amazing is not the technology—it's the marshaling of the resources and the fact that they used this same commonsense expertise to create a structure four hundred and eighty feet high: that implies a confidence that's truly breathtaking."

The Larger Question

We may now understand the how of pyramid building a little better, but what about the mystery of why: what lay behind the epic vision of the Pharaoh's architects? Surely not the mere mastery of technique and logistics which so preoccupies modern researchers and film producers. Above all, we know that the Egyptians were concerned with expressing and maintaining sacred traditions. In these traditions the power of the immortals, the divine status of the dead Pharaoh, and the authority of the state all merged into one—a union that the pyramid itself powerfully symbolized. Indeed, the Pharaoh's unwavering power was strikingly demonstrated in the engineering of his tomb, which called for the rigid control of measurements and angles year after year as the structure rose.

As we know from many ancient texts, the Egyptians visualized the pyramid as a kind of active sacred machine, working together with all the forces of nature to transform the soul of the Pharaoh. Moreover, this transformation happened not only once, at the Pharaoh's funeral, but every morning as the sun rose. Each night the King's spirit merged with the sun and the body of Osiris in the underworld, and at dawn it burst forth to reanimate all living things.

So the pyramid likely represented much more than a personal passport to heaven for the Pharaoh; it was probably built to reflect and sustain the entire cosmos. The near perfection achieved by Cheops' architects only makes sense given a belief system in which every spell, every invocation, had to be performed perfectly to guarantee eternal life for all. Precision was never pursued as an end in itself, as it is in today's world, but was interwoven with the magic of the daily moment of rebirth.

Stonehenge Is the Relic of an Ancient European Culture

James Trefil

Constructed over a twelve-hundred-year period between 3000 B.C. and 1800 B.C., Stonehenge is one of the most enigmatic monuments ever built. That the structure was built at all is, at the very least, a testimony to the dedication of an unknown group of ancient peoples. Its stunning alignment with astronomical phenomena, discovered by astronomer Gerald S. Hawkins in 1963, has made Stonehenge an even greater mystery than it already was. Some even argue that an ancient human civilization could not have possibly built anything of such architectural and astronomical sophistication—that it must have been the work of extraterrestrials or other unknown forces.

James Trefil, Clarence J. Robinson Professor of Physics at George Mason University and author of twenty-one books covering a variety of science topics, argues that Stonehenge is an astronomical calendar that represents the efforts of an

James Trefil, "Architects of Time," *Astronomy*, vol. 27, September 1999, p. 48.

ancient civilization to predict and comprehend time. Citing carbon dating evidence, he argues that it was built in three phases—each time improved to better serve its function. According to Trefil, its construction would have probably been well within the means of an ancient civilization; he cites a BBC television documentary in which a group of young men, equipped with primitive tools, was able to transport stones of a similar size and weight.

We have a sense that time is measured in terms of repeating processes in nature—the swing of a pendulum, the turning of Earth, the stately progression of the seasons. When it comes to measuring time, human beings have traditionally tried to find a steadily repeating process to serve as a fundamental definition—the "tick" of the clock.

The first processes that people used as timekeepers were astronomical. In fact three separate astronomical processes make perfectly good "clocks." One is the rotation of Earth around its own axis, which gives us the unit of time we call the day. Another is the time that it takes Earth to move in its orbit around the sun, which defines the year. Finally, although we no longer use it very much, there is a third clock in the sky that moves through 29.5 days—a synodic month—the period it takes for the moon to run through all its phases.

No one knows exactly when the first human being figured out that you could tell time by watching the heavens. Some archaeologists have contended that marks on 20,000-year-old bones taken from Africa and Europe are humanity's first attempt to keep track of the lunar month. A skeptic (and there are many) looking at the same bones might simply see something that had been used as a knife sharpener. Whether or not Ice Age people kept formal astronomical calendars is very much an open issue. We do know that people in societies without writing or iron tools were capable of doing so.

On the plains of Wiltshire, south of London, there is a remarkable monument to the ability of human beings to keep track of time by using the stars. It is called Stonehenge, which means "hanging stones." I can remember going there when I was a student at Oxford in the 1960s and walking around them as I wished, in the days when it was simply a bunch of stones sitting out on the plain. It's too bad that today, in order to protect the monument, the British government has had to fence the stones and keep visitors at a distance.

How Stonehenge Was Built

The oldest part of Stonehenge, called Stonehenge I, consists of little more than a circular ditch dug in the chalky soil of the Salisbury plain, with the soil taken from the ditch piled up to make an embankment about 6 feet tall. This part of the monument is some 320 feet across. Inside this large circle are the things that we normally think of as Stonehenge proper—circles of stones that once stood upright, and most photogenic of all, the large horseshoe arrangements of standing stones at the center. These last, the so-called trilithons, consist of upright stones supporting horizontal lintels, and the largest of them weighs in around 45 tons.

Legends about the origin and purpose of Stonehenge are legion. It has, for example, been attributed to Druids, and modern-day Druids in England call it theirs. We know, however, that it was built long before the Celtic invasion of Great Britain, so although the Druids might have used it, they certainly did not build it. There are other legends ascribing it to Julius Caesar, Merlin the Magician (who flew the stones in from Ireland), and extraterrestrials in flying saucers. Actually, you do not have to go to these lengths to explain Stonehenge. British students have shown that stones such as those in the monument can easily be moved around by a team of strong young men—one method featured on a BBC television program involved tying a stone to a sleigh and then pulling the sleigh over log rollers.

Several questions that come quickly to mind about a monument such as Stonehenge: Who built it? When was it built? How was it built? Why was it built?

When Stonehenge Was Built

You must answer the "when" question before you can make much progress on the others. Carbon dating comes to the rescue. The idea behind this is simple. The upper atmosphere of Earth is constantly being bombarded by high-energy particles—called cosmic rays—and when they hit the atmosphere they break up the nuclei they encounter, creating neutrons in the process. Some of these neutrons strike the nuclei of ordinary nitrogen atoms, creating an atom with a nucleus that has 6 protons and 8 neutrons. This atom is chemically identical to ordinary carbon (which has 6 protons and 6 neutrons) but weighs a little more. It is called carbon-14 to distinguish it from its more common sibling, carbon-12. Carbon-14 is radioactive, and in 5,860 years half the carbon-14 nuclei in any collection will have undergone radioactive decay back to nitrogen-14.

While it's around, carbon-14 is taken into the bodies of living things just like carbon-12. Thus, when any living thing dies, it holds a certain amount of carbon-14. The subsequent decay of the nuclei gives us a kind of clock that tells us when that particular thing died and stopped taking in carbon. If we found a piece of leather with half of the carbon-14 with which it started, we would know that the leather was made from an animal that died about 5,860 years ago. In the 1950s, Harold Urey of the University of Chicago developed the carbon-dating technique, and it was immediately put to use by paleontologists and archaeologists everywhere around the world. . . .

Using this technique, scholars now date the bank-and-ditch structure to around 3000 B.C., the first stones to about 2600 B.C., the large standing stones to about 2100 B.C., and the last adjustments to the structure to about 1800 B.C. Thus, the construction of Stonehenge took 1,200 years—much longer than Europeans have inhabited North America. It was built by successive waves of immigrants to southern England. Most of them did not have metal tools or a written language. Anthropologists are also in agreement that quarrying, transporting, and erecting the stones would be well within the technical capabilities of the people who lived around Stonehenge while it was being built. There is, in other words, no need to invoke either Merlin the Magician or extraterrestrials in flying saucers!

Why Stonehenge Was Built

With the when, who, and how disposed of, we can turn to the more interesting question of why in the world anyone would go through all the trouble of setting those huge stones upright on the plains of Salisbury. It is almost certain that the only thing that could inspire this much effort over that period of time would be a religion or religious practices, and most scholars accept that Stonehenge was first and foremost the site of religious and/or civic celebrations. But is that all there is?

In 1963, British astronomer Gerald Hawkins published an article in *Nature*, followed by a book, *Stonehenge Decoded*. He proposed a rather startling hypothesis for at least one purpose of this ancient monument. Having grown up in the neighborhood of Stonehenge, Hawkins began his analysis by recalling that when he stood in the center of the stones as a boy, he felt as if the builders, by the placement of the stones, had wanted to force him to look in certain directions. Using the best computer available at the time, Hawkins fed these lines of sight into a program designed to see whether they matched the lines of sight to any significant astronomical events.

Fully 24 of the lines pointed to significant astronomical events. The most famous of these are the alignments that point to the spot on the horizon at which the sun rises on the summer and winter solstices, but there were many lines pointing to the rising and setting of the full moon nearest those dates as well. Hawkins discovered Stonehenge was not only a religious site, it also was an astronomical observatory and calendar. Stonehenge was a device by which the builders could tell, on an annual basis, when Earth arrived at a certain point in its orbit around the sun.

This observation about the astronomical nature of Stonehenge was greeted with great excitement by the astronomical community—it was instrumental in spawning a new field, called archaeoastronomy, devoted to the study of the astronomical function of ancient monuments. Over the years, astronomers have found similar purposes for many other ancient monuments in the old and new world.

Hawkins' discovery also caused what my daughters would call a "hissy fit" among archaeologists. There is nothing that annoys a scientist more than having an old problem in his or her field solved by someone from outside. (If you doubt this comment, just think about the reaction of paleontologists to the discovery by Luis and Walter Alvarez that the extinction of the dinosaurs was caused by the impact of a large meteor on the surface of the planet.) This reaction usually manifested itself in peevish comments by archaeologists to the effect that Stonehenge was more than just an astronomical observatory, but had some social function as well.

The construction of Stonehenge symbolizes humanity's attempt to cope with the passage of time through the use of astronomy. Perhaps more importantly, Stonehenge illustrates one of the most important things about the universe in which we live—that it is regular and predictable. It would scarcely be worthwhile for people to haul huge stones over miles of rough terrain to provide a ceremonial observation of the summer solstice if that solstice appeared in a different part of the sky every year. By its sheer bulk, Stonehenge reminds us that the basic premise of science (that we can understand and predict the universe that we live in) is a valid one.

The Easter Island Statues Were Built by a Lost Polynesian Civilization

Jared Diamond

Resting more than two thousand miles away from the nearest population center in a seldom-traveled area of the Pacific Ocean, Easter Island is one of the most remote places on Earth. The island is decorated by giant stone face carvings, called *moai*, that were presumably carved and then moved into place by the island's ancient inhabitants. Yet on this island, there is no sign of ropes or timber—essential tools for any workers attempting to move stone objects the size of *moai*. According to Jared Diamond, professor of physiology at the UCLA Medical School and author of eight books on a wide range of topics, archaeologists have found

Jared Diamond, "Easter's End," *Discover*, vol. 16, August 1995, p. 62. Copyright © 1995 by Discover Magazine. Reproduced by permission of the author.

a disturbing answer to this riddle: The island's residents did possess ropes and timber at the time the statues were built (roughly A.D. 1200–1500), but then gradually drove the plant species that provided them with those supplies—and the ecosystem that supported their own survival—into extinction. By the time Dutch explorer Jacob Roggeveen discovered the island in the early eighteenth century, many of its natural resources had been depleted.

Easter Island, with an area of only 64 square miles, is the world's most isolated scrap of habitable land. It lies in the Pacific Ocean more than 2,000 miles west of the nearest continent (South America), 1,400 miles from even the nearest habitable island (Pitcairn). Its subtropical location and latitude—at 27 degrees south, it is approximately as far below the equator as Houston is north of it—help give it a rather mild climate, while its volcanic origins make its soil fertile. In theory, this combination of blessings should have made Easter a miniature paradise, remote from problems that beset the rest of the world.

The island derives its name from its "discovery" by the Dutch explorer Jacob Roggeveen, on Easter (April 5) in 1722. Roggeveen's first impression was not of a paradise but of a wasteland: "We originally, from a further distance, have considered the said Easter Island as sandy; the reason for that is this, that we counted as sand the withered grass, hay, or other scorched and burnt vegetation, because its wasted appearance could give no other impression than of a singular poverty and barrenness."

The island Roggeveen saw was a grassland without a single tree or bush over ten feet high. Modern botanists have identified only 47 species of higher plants native to

Easter, most of them grasses, sedges, and ferns. The list includes just two species of small trees and two of woody
shrubs. With such flora, the islanders Roggeveen encountered had no source of real firewood to warm themselves
during Easter's cool, wet, windy winters. Their native animals included nothing larger than insects, not even a single
species of native bat, land bird, land snail, or lizard. For domestic animals, they had only chickens.

European visitors throughout the eighteenth and early
nineteenth centuries estimated Easter's human population
at about 2,000, a modest number considering the island's
fertility. As Captain James Cook recognized during his brief
visit in 1774, the islanders were Polynesians (a Tahitian man
accompanying Cook was able to converse with them). Yet
despite the Polynesians' well-deserved fame as a great seafaring people, the Easter Islanders who came out to Roggeveen's and Cook's ships did so by swimming or paddling
canoes that Roggeveen described as "bad and frail." Their
craft, he wrote, were "put together with manifold small
planks and light inner timbers, which they cleverly stitched
together with very fine twisted threads. . . . But as they lack
the knowledge and particularly the materials for caulking
and making tight the great number of seams of the canoes,
these are accordingly very leaky, for which reason they are
compelled to spend half the time in bailing." The canoes,
only ten feet long, held at most two people, and only three
or four canoes were observed on the entire island.

With such flimsy craft, Polynesians could never have col-
onized Easter from even the nearest island, nor could
[Easter Islanders] have traveled far offshore to fish. The islanders Roggeveen met were totally isolated, unaware that
other people existed. Investigators in all the years since his
visit have discovered no trace of the islanders having any
outside contacts: not a single Easter Island rock or product

has turned up elsewhere, nor has anything been found on the island that could have been brought by anyone other than the original settlers or the Europeans. Yet the people living on Easter claimed memories of visiting the uninhabited Sala y Gomez reef 260 miles away, far beyond the range of the leaky canoes seen by Roggeveen. How did the islanders' ancestors reach that reef from Easter, or reach Easter from anywhere else?

The Mystery of the Statues

Easter Island's most famous feature is its huge stone statues, more than 200 of which once stood on massive stone platforms lining the coast. At least 700 more, in all stages of completion, were abandoned in quarries or on ancient roads between the quarries and the coast, as if the carvers and moving crews had thrown down their tools and walked off the job. Most of the erected statues were carved in a single quarry and then somehow transported as far as six miles—despite heights as great as 33 feet and weights up to 82 tons. The abandoned statues, meanwhile, were as much as 65 feet tall and weighed up to 270 tons. The stone platforms were equally gigantic: up to 500 feet long and 10 feet high, with facing slabs weighing up to 10 tons.

Roggeveen himself quickly recognized the problem the statues posed: "The stone images at first caused us to be struck with astonishment," he wrote, "because we could not comprehend how it was possible that these people, who are devoid of heavy thick timber for making any machines, as well as strong ropes, nevertheless had been able to erect such images." Roggeveen might have added that the islanders had no wheels, no draft animals, and no source of power except their own muscles. How did they transport the giant statues for miles, even before erecting them? To deepen the mystery, the statues were still standing in 1770, but by 1864 all of them had been pulled down, by the islanders themselves. Why then did they carve them in the first place? And why did they stop?

The statues imply a society very different from the one Roggeveen saw in 1722. Their sheer number and size suggest a population much larger than 2,000 people. What became of everyone? Furthermore, that society must have been highly organized. Easter's resources were scattered across the island: the best stone for the statues was quarried at Rano Raraku near Easter's northeast end; red stone, used for large crowns adorning some of the statues, was quarried at Puna Pau, inland in the southwest; stone carving tools came mostly from Aroi in the northwest. Meanwhile, the best farmland lay in the south and east, and the best fishing grounds on the north and west coasts. Extracting and redistributing all those goods required complex political organization. What happened to that organization, and how could it ever have arisen in such a barren landscape?

Easter Island's mysteries have spawned volumes of speculation for more than two and a half centuries. Many Europeans were incredulous that Polynesians—commonly characterized as "mere savages" could have created the statues or the beautifully constructed stone platforms. In the 1950s, Heyerdahl argued that Polynesia must have been settled by advanced societies of American Indians, who in turn must have received civilization across the Atlantic from more advanced societies of the Old World. Heyerdahl's raft voyages aimed to prove the feasibility of such prehistoric transoceanic contacts. In the 1960s the Swiss writer Erich von Daniken, an ardent believer in Earth visits by extraterrestrial astronauts, went further, claiming that Easter's statues were the work of intelligent beings who owned ultramodern tools, became stranded on Easter, and were finally rescued.

A Native Culture

Heyerdahl and von Daniken both brushed aside over-whelming evidence that the Easter Islanders were typical Polynesians derived from Asia rather than from the Americas and that their culture (including their statues) grew out of Polynesian culture. Their language was Polynesian, as Cook had already concluded. Specifically, they spoke an eastern Polynesian dialect related to Hawaiian and Marquesan, a dialect isolated since about A.D. 400, as estimated from slight differences in vocabulary. Their fishhooks and stone adzes resembled early Marquesan models. DNA extracted from 12 Easter Island skeletons was also shown to be Polynesian. The islanders grew bananas, taro, sweet potatoes, sugarcane, and paper mulberry—typical Polynesian crops, mostly of Southeast Asian origin. Their sole domestic animal, the chicken, was also typically Polynesian and ultimately Asian, as were the rats that arrived as stowaways in the canoes of the first settlers.

What happened to those settlers? The fanciful theories of the past must give way to evidence gathered by hardworking practitioners in three fields: archeology, pollen analysis, and paleontology.

Modern archeological excavations on Easter have continued since Heyerdahl's 1955 expedition. The earliest radiocarbon dates associated with human activities are around A.D. 400 to 700, in reasonable agreement with the approximate settlement date of 400 estimated by linguists. The period of statue construction peaked around 1200 to 1500, with few if any statues erected thereafter. Densities of archeological sites suggest a large population; an estimate of 7,000 people is widely quoted by archeologists, but other estimates range up to 20,000, which does not seem implausible for an island of Easter's area and fertility.

Destroying the Tools

Archeologists have also enlisted surviving islanders in experiments aimed at figuring out how the statues might have been carved and erected. Twenty people, using only stone chisels, could have carved even the largest completed statue within a year. Given enough timber and fiber for making ropes, teams of at most a few hundred people could have loaded the statues onto wooden sleds, dragged them over lubricated wooden tracks or rollers, and used logs as levers to maneuver them into a standing position. Rope could have been made from the fiber of a small native tree, related to the linden, called the hauhau. However, that tree is now extremely scarce on Easter, and hauling one statue would have required hundreds of yards of rope. Did Easter's now barren landscape once support the necessary trees?

That question can be answered by the technique of pollen analysis, which involves boring out a column of sediment from a swamp or pond, with the most recent deposits at the top and relatively more ancient deposits at the bottom. The absolute age of each layer can be dated by radiocarbon methods. Then begins the hard work: examining tens of thousands of pollen grains under a microscope, counting them, and identifying the plant species that produced each one by comparing the grains with modern pollen from known plant species. For Easter Island, the bleary-eyed scientists who performed that task were John Flenley, now at Massey University in New Zealand, and Sarah King of the University of Hull in England.

Flenley and King's heroic efforts were rewarded by the striking new picture that emerged of Easter's prehistoric landscape. For at least 30,000 years before human arrival and during the early years of Polynesian settlement, Easter was not a wasteland at all. Instead, a subtropical forest of trees and woody bushes towered over a ground layer of shrubs, herbs, ferns, and grasses. In the forest grew tree daisies, the rope-yielding hauhau tree, and the toromiro tree, which furnishes a dense, mesquite-like firewood. The most common tree in the forest was a species of palm now absent on Easter but formerly so abundant that the bottom strata of the sediment column were packed with its pollen. The Easter Island palm was closely related to the still-surviving Chilean wine palm, which grows up to 82 feet tall and 6 feet in diameter. The tall, unbranched trunks of the Easter Island palm would have been ideal for transporting and erecting statues and constructing large canoes. The palm would also have been a valuable food source, since its Chilean relative yields edible nuts as well as sap from which Chileans make sugar, syrup, honey, and wine.

What did the first settlers of Easter Island eat when they were not glutting themselves on the local equivalent of maple syrup? Recent excavations by David Steadman, of the New York State Museum at Albany, have yielded a picture of Easter's original animal world as surprising as Flenley and King's picture of its plant world. Steadman's expectations for Easter were conditioned by his experiences elsewhere in Polynesia, where fish are overwhelmingly the main food at archeological sites, typically accounting for more than 90 percent of the bones in ancient Polynesian garbage heaps. Easter, though, is too cool for the coral reefs beloved by fish, and its cliff-girded coastline permits shallow-water fishing in only a few places. Less than a quarter of the bones in its early garbage heaps (from the period 900 to 1300) belonged to fish; instead, nearly one-third of all bones came from porpoises. . . .

In addition to porpoise meat, Steadman found, the early Polynesian settlers were feasting on seabirds. For those birds, Easter's remoteness and lack of predators made it an ideal haven as a breeding site, at least until humans arrived. Among the prodigious numbers of seabirds that bred on Easter were albatross, boobies, frigate birds, fulmars, petrels, prions, shearwaters, storm petrels, terns, and tropic birds. . . .

The Fall of a Culture

Such evidence lets us imagine the island onto which Easter's first Polynesian colonists stepped ashore some 1,600 years ago, after a long canoe voyage from eastern Polynesia. They found themselves in a pristine paradise. What then happened to it? The pollen grains and the bones yield a grim answer.

Pollen records show that destruction of Easter's forests was well under way by the year 800, just a few centuries after the start of human settlement. Then charcoal from wood fires came to fill the sediment cores, while pollen of palms and other trees and woody shrubs decreased or disappeared, and pollen of the grasses that replaced the forest became more abundant. Not long after 1400 the palm finally became extinct, not only as a result of being chopped down but also because the now ubiquitous rats prevented its regeneration: of the dozens of preserved palm nuts discovered in caves on Easter, all had been chewed by rats and could no longer germinate. While the hauhau tree did not become extinct in Polynesian times, its numbers declined drastically until there weren't enough left to make ropes from. By the time Heyerdahl visited Easter, only a single, nearly dead toromiro tree remained on the island, and even that lone mirror has now disappeared. (Fortunately, the toromiro still grows in botanical gardens elsewhere.)

The fifteenth century marked the end not only for Easter's palm but for the forest itself. Its doom had been approaching as people cleared land to plant gardens; as they felled trees to build canoes, to transport and erect statues, and to burn; as rats devoured seeds; and probably as the native birds died out that had pollinated the trees' flowers and dispersed their fruit. The overall picture is among the most extreme examples of forest destruction anywhere in the world: the whole forest gone, and most of its tree species extinct.

The destruction of the island's animals was as extreme as that of the forest: without exception, every species of native land bird became extinct. Even shellfish were overexploited, until people had to settle for small sea snails instead of larger cowries. Porpoise bones disappeared abruptly from garbage heaps around 1500; no one could harpoon porpoises anymore, since the trees used for constructing the big seagoing canoes no longer existed. The colonies of more than half of the seabird species breeding on Easter or on its offshore islets were wiped out.

In place of these meat supplies, the Easter Islanders intensified their production of chickens, which had been only an occasional food item. They also turned to the largest remaining meat source available: humans, whose bones became common in late Easter Island garbage heaps. Oral traditions of the islanders are rife with cannibalism; the most inflammatory taunt that could be snarled at an enemy was "The flesh of your mother sticks between my teeth." With no wood available to cook these new goodies, the islanders resorted to sugarcane scraps, grass, and sedges to fuel their fires.

A World Lost

All these strands of evidence can be wound into a coherent narrative of a society's decline and fall. The first Polynesian colonists found themselves on an island with fertile soil, abundant food, bountiful building materials, ample lebensraum, and all the prerequisites for comfortable living. They prospered and multiplied.

After a few centuries, they began erecting stone statues on

platforms, like the ones their Polynesian forebears had carved. With passing years, the statues and platforms became larger and larger, and the statues began sporting ten-ton red crowns—probably in an escalating spiral of one-upmanship, as rival clans tried to surpass each other with shows of wealth and power. (In the same way, successive Egyptian pharaohs built ever-larger pyramids. Today Hollywood movie moguls near my home in Los Angeles are displaying their wealth and power by building ever more ostentatious mansions. Tycoon Marvin Davis topped previous moguls with plans for a 50,000-square-foot house, so now Aaron Spelling has topped Davis with a 56,000-square-foot house. All that those buildings lack to make the message explicit are ten-ton red crowns.) On Easter, as in modern America, society was held together by a complex political system to redistribute locally available resources and to integrate the economies of different areas.

Eventually Easter's growing population was cutting the forest more rapidly than the forest was regenerating. The people used the land for gardens and the wood for fuel, canoes, and houses—and, of course, for lugging statues. As forest disappeared, the islanders ran out of timber and rope to transport and erect their statues. Life became more uncomfortable—springs and streams dried up, and wood was no longer available for fires.

People also found it harder to fill their stomachs, as land birds, large sea snails, and many seabirds disappeared. Because timber for building seagoing canoes vanished, fish catches declined and porpoises disappeared from the table. Crop yields also declined, since deforestation allowed the soil to be eroded by rain and wind, dried by the sun, and its nutrients to be leeched from it. Intensified chicken production and cannibalism replaced only part of all those lost foods. Preserved statuettes with sunken cheeks and visible ribs suggest that people were starving.

With the disappearance of food surpluses, Easter Island could no longer feed the chiefs, bureaucrats, and priests who had kept a complex society running. Surviving islanders described to early European visitors how local chaos replaced centralized government and a warrior class took over from the hereditary chiefs. The stone points of spears and daggers, made by the warriors during their heyday in the 1600s and 1700s, still litter the ground of Easter today. By around 1700, the population began to crash toward between one-quarter and one-tenth of its former number. People took to living in caves for protection against their enemies. Around 1770 rival clans started to topple each other's statues, breaking the heads off. By 1864 the last statue had been thrown down and desecrated.

Chapter 3

Fact or Fiction?

Evidence That
UFO Landing
Sites Exist

An Alien Spacecraft Crashed in New Mexico in 1947

Kevin D. Randle

An unidentified flying object crashed near Roswell, New Mexico, in July 1947. After claiming for fifty years that the object was a weather balloon, the U.S. Air Force acknowledged a cover-up and announced that the crash was the result of Project Mogul, a spy microphone designed to detect Soviet nuclear missile tests. While skeptics (and some former believers) accept this as a satisfactory explanation for the Roswell cover-up, many reject this new account. After all, some argue, if the U.S. military has already lied once about the Roswell incident, how does one know that they are not lying again?

Kevin D. Randle is a retired air force intelligence officer and author who has written forty-seven books on a wide range of topics (thirteen of them dealing specifically with UFOs or alien contact). In this excerpt from his book *Case MJ-12: The True Story Behind the Government's UFO Conspir-*

acies (2002), he argues that an extraterrestrial spacecraft crashed near Roswell, New Mexico, in 1947.

According to the *Roswell Daily Record*, on July 8, 1947, Colonel William "Butch" Blanchard, commanding officer of the 509th Bomb Group, announced through his public relations office that they, meaning the 509th, had "captured" a crashed flying saucer on a ranch outside of Roswell, New Mexico. The story was reported around the country that afternoon. There were few details given. The local sheriff, George A. Wilcox, was named, as was Major Jesse A. Marcel, the Air Intelligence officer of the 509th. Mack Brazel, the local rancher who had apparently made the discovery, was not mentioned by name.

Within hours, Brigadier General Roger M. Ramey, the commanding officer of the 8th Air Force, parent unit to the 509th, held a press conference at the Fort Worth Army Air Field to announce that a weather balloon had been responsible for the wreckage. Material recovered near Roswell was taken to Fort Worth, where the 8th Air Force was headquartered, and identified, first by Ramey and later by a weather officer, Warrant Officer Irving Newton, as a neoprene balloon and the remains of a rawin radar reflector. In 1947, that was the end of the story. After all, reporters had seen the weather balloon, the radar target, and heard a general tell them that the debris brought to his office and displayed there was all that had been found. . . .

Roswell Revealed

Then, in early 1978, Jesse A. Marcel surfaced. He told researchers Stan Friedman and Len Stringfield that he was the man who had picked up pieces of a flying saucer some thirty years earlier. He told them it had happened near Roswell; he wasn't sure of the exact year, but it was in the late 1940s. He provided a few details, the most important, he was one of the men on the scene, he had been the Air Intelligence officer, and he was willing to tell his story on the record. His name could be used. Suddenly, anonymity had a name.

It took no time for more details to be found. A search of newspaper files, beginning with the Arnold sighting on June 24, yielded results almost immediately. Beginning with the July 8 newspapers, articles from New Mexico were carried in a number of later editions and continued for several days. On July 9 many newspapers carried pictures of Jesse Marcel crouched near the remains of a blackened weather balloon and a badly damaged radar target. With his picture in the newspaper, his position with the 509th Bomb Group identified, and the date confirmed, it was now possible to begin serious research.

[Ufologist] Stan Friedman is fond of telling people that he was the first to identify some of the important players in the case. According to him, he called the offices of the *Roswell Daily Record* hoping to learn if any of the people involved in the 1947 story still lived in Roswell and if the newspaper reporters might help him locate some of them. Proving that sometimes things are extremely easy for those who stir the pot, Friedman learned that Walter Haut's wife worked at the newspaper office. Haut was the 509th's public relations officer who wrote the original press release back in 1947.

Len Stringfield talked to Jesse Marcel, and proving that it's sometimes a small world, learned that he and Marcel had served on the same island in the Pacific, doing the same basic job, during the Second World War. Marcel told Stringfield, as he'd told Friedman, about picking up pieces of a flying saucer. Stringfield, in his 1978 Mutual UFO Network

(MUFON) Symposium paper, announced, for the first time, the results of his interview with Marcel, suggesting that Marcel had found physical evidence of a flying saucer. . . .

The Marcel Account

Marcel provided information to suggest that something had exploded in the air, and said he was dispatched, by the 509th commanding officer, Colonel Blanchard, to investigate. According to Stringfield, Marcel told him that "he found many metal fragments and what appeared to be 'parchment' strewn in a 1-mile-square area. 'The metal fragments,' said the Major, 'varied in size up to 6 inches in length, but were of the thickness of tinfoil. The fragments were unusual . . . because they were of great strength. They could not be bent or broken, no matter what pressure we applied by hand.'"

After the initial excitement, there were suggestions by skeptics, debunkers, journalists, and UFO researchers that Marcel had handled bits of a classified balloon, which of course explained the strange material. Stringfield then called Marcel and on October 5, 1979, Stringfield asked him specifically about finding a balloon, regardless of type, classification, or material. Marcel told Stringfield, "The material I gathered did not resemble anything off a balloon. A balloon, of any kind, could not have exploded and spread its debris over such a broad area. . . . I was told later that a military team from my base was sent to rake the entire area."

So, unlike the tales reported in the past, filled with unidentified sources at some unspecified location, this tale of a flying saucer crash had names. Major Jesse Marcel was a real person who, in July 1947, was the intelligence officer in Roswell, just as he had claimed. He told those who called to interview him that he was the right man, his picture was in the newspaper, and he had picked up pieces of a flying saucer. Other documentation, including his military records, secured through the Army Personnel Record Center in St. Louis, verified the claim that he was an Army officer assigned to Roswell. However, those records could not confirm that a flying saucer had been found.

About the craft he had found and the wreckage he'd examined, he told researchers, "It was something that came to Earth but not something that was built on Earth.". . .

The Brazel Account

Mack Brazel, according to the July 9 issue of the *Roswell Daily Record*, was the anonymous rancher mentioned in the July 8 issue of the newspaper. He had come into town to tell the sheriff, and the military, that something had scattered quite a bit of debris in one of the pastures on the ranch that he managed. According to the newspaper:

W.W. Brazel, 48, Lincoln County rancher living 30 miles southeast of Corona, today told his story of finding what the army at first described as a flying disk, but the publicity which attended his find caused him to add that if he ever found anything else short of a bomb he sure wasn't going to say anything about it. . . .

Brazel related that on June 14 he and an 8-year-old son, Vernon, were about 7 or 8 miles from the ranch house of the J.B. Foster ranch, which he operates, when they came upon a large area of bright wreckage made up on [sic] rubber strips, tinfoil, a rather tough paper and sticks.

At the time Brazel was in a hurry to get his round made and he did not pay much attention to it. But he did remark about what he had seen and on July 4 he, his wife, Vernon, and a daughter, Betty, age 14, went back to the spot and gathered up quite a bit of the debris.

The next day he first heard about the flying disks, and he wondered if what he had found might be remnants of one of these.

Monday he came to town to sell some wool, and while here he went to see Sheriff George Wilcox and "whispered kinda confidential like" that he might have found a flying disk.

Wilcox got in touch with the Roswell Army Air Field, and Maj. Jesse A. Marcel and a man in plainclothes accompanied him home, where they picked up the rest of the pieces of the "disk" and went to his home to reconstruct it.

According to Brazel, they simply could not reconstruct it all. They tried to make a kite out of it but could not do that and could not find any way to put it back together so that it would fit.

Then Major Marcel brought it to Roswell, and that was the last he heard of it until the story broke that he had found a flying disk. . . .

"The Air Force Asked Him to Take an Oath"

Brazel died in 1963, long before anyone began a serious investigation into the crash, but members of his family, who had lived in New Mexico for generations, were still there. Bill Brazel, Jr., was located and reluctantly agreed to provide information. In February 1989 he told me, "My dad found this thing and told me a little bit about it. Not much . . . because the Air Force asked him to take an oath that he wouldn't tell anybody in detail about it. And my dad was such a guy that he went to his grave and he never told anybody."

But Bill Brazel had done more than just listen to his father tell the abbreviated tale of the crashed saucer. According to him, "I found a few bits and pieces later on."

Unfortunately, again according to Brazel, he didn't hang on to them very long. Word reached the Air Force that Brazel had some samples of the material and they came out to take them. "They didn't confiscate it. They put it in such a way that I should give it to them. . . ."

I asked Brazel to describe the material to me. He said, "There were three items involved. Something on the order of balsa wood and something on the order of heavy gauge monofilament fishing line and a little piece of . . . it wasn't really aluminum foil and it wasn't really lead foil but it was on that order."

General descriptions of the material didn't seem unusual, but the details were. For example, the "fishing line" Brazel described had the properties of fiber optics. He said that if you shined a light in one end, it would come out the other, no matter how the line was twisted or bent. And concerning the tinfoil, he said it could be folded, bent, creased, or even wadded into a ball, and when you let go of it, it returned to its original shape: "It would flatten out and it was just as smooth as ever. Not a crinkle or anything in it."

He also talked about the piece of debris that he described as a small bit of wood and lightweight, with no real density, but extremely tough. It was light brown in color and, according to Brazel, had no stratification. He had tried to whittle on it with his pocket knife because he wanted to see if there were internal markings, but was unable to cut or scratch the material. He said that he couldn't even get a small shaving from it. . . .

Censoring the Media

George "Jud" Roberts was the minority owner of radio station KGFL in 1947. He did not participate in the interview [KGFL conducted] with Brazel, but Roberts was at the station when the telephone calls came in from Washington, D.C., Roberts told me, on more than one occasion, that he had received calls from the Federal Communications Commission telling him that if KGFL broadcast the [first] interview with Brazel, the station would lose its license. They could all look for new jobs.

Roberts, and others, suggested that there were also telephone calls from various members of the New Mexico congressional delegation. They urged him and others at the station not to broadcast the interview. Again there were threats about the retention of their license.

Mack Brazel was then taken to the newspaper office to give his [second] "official" interview. According to a half dozen of his friends who saw him in Roswell that day, he was escorted by several military officers. They waited around as he gave the new story that talked of balsa wood sticks and a weather balloon to the newspaper reporters, including two from the Associated Press, then took him on to the radio station. There, Frank Joyce put him on the air live, and Brazel told the revised story of the weather balloon and kitelike appendage. Joyce told me later that Brazel was bothered by this, but that he stuck to the new party line.

Bill Brazel told me that he read about his father's problems in the newspaper in Albuquerque, where he was living at the time. Bill realized that there was no one else at the ranch and that his father would need some help. He drove down on the following weekend, and when he arrived, his father was still gone. By Bill Brazel's calculation, his father was in Roswell, and in the hands of the military, for about six days.

Marian Strickland, a Brazel neighbor, told me that Mack Brazel sat in her kitchen, drinking coffee and complaining to her husband Lyman that he, Brazel, had been kept in jail by the military. Technically that wasn't true. He had been held in the guest house, as confirmed by Edwin Easley, but if you're not allowed to leave, if there are guards on the door keeping you inside, then it isn't that much different from jail.

Project Mogul and the Weather Balloon

What all of this suggests is that something extraordinary fell outside of Roswell in July 1947. The military wouldn't have gone to the effort it had if there wasn't a good reason for it. The remains of a weather balloon, no matter what the source, were just that—the remains of a weather balloon. Soviet spies, foreign agents, and even American industry couldn't have learned much in the way of national secrets by the recovery of a weather balloon. Nor could they learn much about Project Mogul, the so-called secret balloon project, from the photographs of balloons published in the newspapers.

Maybe this is the place to point out that the Project Mogul explanation for the debris recovery offered by the Air Force in 1994 does not cover this sort of event. In 1947, according to the latest information, Mogul was highly classified. Charles Moore, an engineer on the Mogul team, told me that he didn't even know the name of the project until 1992. This suggests that the extraordinary efforts documented by the newspapers, of military activity in 1947, could have been intended to hide the classified nature of Mogul.

The problem with that theory is that just two days later, on July 10, 1947, pictures of a Mogul launch were published in newspapers around the country. While the purpose of Mogul was classified, the equipment used and the balloon array trains being launched from the Alamogordo, New Mexico, area were not. In other words, had Mogul been the explanation, there would have been no reason to hide the recovered debris or the fact that the balloons were being launched. Nor would teams of military personnel have been guarding the sites holding people incommunicado on the base. Frankly, even in 1947, Mogul wasn't that important. . . .

The New Roswell Investigation

Only during the last twenty years, as new witnesses were identified and new documents discovered, has the Roswell case began to take on significance. The publication of *The Roswell Incident*, in 1980, was the first break, though the book was ignored by many in the UFO community. There was some discussion of it, but as had happened in 1947, there wasn't much interest. J.P. Cahn's 1952 story, which destroyed the Aztec UFO crash tale, was in the back of everyone's mind.

But *The Roswell Incident* did generate interest. Then in 1988, the J. Allen Hynek Center of UFO Studies (CUFOS) became more involved in the Roswell case. Although assuming that there would be a mundane explanation for the crash, it was decided that more work needed to be done. With fifty or sixty people named as having some sort of information, both first- and secondhand data, and with some indications that the case might have potential, CUFOS initiated its own investigation. . . .

Looking for Witnesses

The first place to begin, to my way of thinking, was with Bill Brazel. Knowing that he lived in New Mexico, his telephone number was easy to find, and a preliminary call suggested that the material published about him in *The Roswell Incident* was basically correct. But he was reluctant to say anything else on the telephone, and I needed more information. I was able to arrange a meeting with him in Carizozo, New Mexico, in February 1989. At that point it became clear to me that something extraordinary had happened. His description of the debris and of the visit by the military officers to obtain the scraps of material he'd found after the event said that this was much more important than a weather balloon and radar reflector that had crashed.

Unfortunately, I learned little that was new during that trip. A meeting with Frank Joyce, the former reporter, announcer, and disc jockey on KGFL radio, fell through. Other scheduled meetings with UFO researchers in New Mexico proved to be of little value. And we needed more information.

The investigation, which continued for years, eventually convinced me that something extraterrestrial had fallen near Roswell. Some of the evidence was subtle. For example, I called Major Edwin Easley after learning that he was the provost marshal, and finding his name and telephone number on a reunion listing for former members of the 509th, I asked him about the alleged crash of the UFO. The first words he said to me were a simple, "I can't talk about it."

During that short, initial conversation, he told me several times that he couldn't talk about it and that he'd been sworn to secrecy. Here we were, at the beginning of the 1990s, and Easley believed that an event that had taken place more than forty years earlier was still classified. He couldn't, and wouldn't, talk about it in any detail.

Oaths of Secrecy

Patrick Saunders, the base adjutant in 1947, told me in my first telephone conversation with him that he knew nothing about "the little green men." He made light of the situation, suggesting there was nothing to the story, that he'd heard nothing like it and wondered where the rumors had started.

Had that been the end of it, Saunders would be one of those who went to his grave without revealing a single fact about the case. But though Saunders wanted to honor the oath he took in 1947, he also wanted to share the information with his friends and family. To do so, he bought several copies of The Truth About the UFO Crash at Roswell and sent them to friends. On the flyleaf of one of those books, he wrote: "Here's the truth and I still haven't told anybody anything!"

In fact, every member of Colonel Blanchard's senior staff who was interviewed, with one exception, told researchers that what had fallen outside of Roswell was of extraterrestrial origin. Marcel was the most vocal, providing hours of videotaped and audiotaped interviews, telling people that the craft did not come from Earth.

[Major Edwin] Easley was reluctant to say much of anything, though he suggested to me that the craft had been extraterrestrial. In a telephone call to him in February 1991, I asked him if we were following the right path. He asked what I meant, and I said, "We think it was extraterrestrial."

Easley replied, "Let me put it this way. That's not the wrong path."

The Nazca Lines May Be UFO Landing Aids

Erich von Däniken

Lightly carved into the stone ground of southeastern Peru's *Pampa Colorada* ("red plain") are a series of massive figures and geometric shapes, some hundreds of feet in length and fully visible only from the air. Historians believe that the most recent designs were carved around 200 B.C., almost two thousand years before the Wright brothers invented the airplane. The exact purpose of these drawings (known as the Nazca drawings) remains a mystery. Most anthropologists believe that they had a religious function consistent with known ancient religions of the region (which generally included at least one major sky god), while others argue that they served as an astronomical calendar or were used to mark water routes.

Swiss writer Erich von Däniken, author of the best-selling *Chariots of the Gods?* (1969), believes that many monuments of the ancient world were constructed to honor extraterrestrial visitors or to commemorate their deeds. In this excerpt from *Arrival of the Gods* (1998), von Däniken argues that the Nazca drawings were UFO landing sites decorated by ancient priests who sought the return of their extraterrestrial visitors.

The first time I saw the shape below me I thought I was seeing things—an optical illusion of some kind. I asked the pilot Eduardo to fly over it again . . . and again and again. And as the plane climbed up to 800 metres, I saw the second phenomenon, linked to the first. As well as the usual photos, I took two with an instant-picture camera. Later, sitting in the shade with a cool drink, I stared at the pictures—not yet dreaming that the next day's flight would throw up two even greater surprises.

Complex Geometric Patterns

First I saw a large circle on whose circumference were more than 60 points. Then I perceived within this first circle a second with countless smaller points on its circumference. In the middle were two superimposed rectangles, each divided into eight squares. These squares were divided by crossing lines from each corner, and in the very centre of the form lay a bundle of 16 lines radiating outwards. What was it? On the second photo I noticed that the whole geometrical pattern was enclosed by two giant squares lying diagonally one on top of the other.

My first thought was of a mandala of some kind, such as the Tibetans and Hindus use in the practice of meditation. The North American Indians have something similar, which they call sand-paintings, composed of many geometrical forms and colours. If the complicated geometrical pattern in front of me was some kind of mandala, then it had to be a modern forgery. Or perhaps a teacher had taken a class of pupils to Nazca and got them to do this for a lark. I had taken my photograph in the Palpa mountains, about 12 minutes' flight from the Nazca airstrip. The mountains there are quite arid; the region is like hell on earth. This geometrical form was so complicated and large scale—approximately 500 metres in diameter—that the group of fakers must have spent an awful long time in the sweltering heat. And their foot and car tracks should have been visible. No one goes to hell with slippers on! Not even the Peruvian army—and they would have left the tracks of their vehicles. I stared at the picture again and again. There were individual lines which did not belong to the geometrical form. Later on, when I was able to compare these shots with the photographs taken with other cameras, I saw that the fainter lines belonged to the network of Nazca lines. I asked Eduardo, and other pilots too, to suggest who might have carried out this modern forgery.

'That's not modern, nor fake—it was always there!'

'Then why is it not mentioned in any of the Nazca tourist guides? I don't ever remember seeing a picture of it before,' I said doubtfully.

They told me that, firstly, the diagram was not on the plain of Nazca but in Palpa, and, secondly, no one knew how to explain it. So they kept mum.

A Gigantic Arrow

I couldn't stop thinking about this geometrical form. The next day we flew back there. Only then, from a greater height, did I notice that the first 'mandala' was connected with a second, and then—from a still greater height—with a third. It was extraordinary! I could forget any ideas of a modern forgery—the proportions of the whole thing were enough to discount that possibility. All three forms together spread over more than a kilometre. In addition—and that made the whole thing still more mysterious—there was a geological cleft running through the middle of the pattern. It began at a corner of the inner rectangle, broadened out, then passed through the two circles and out beyond the enclosing square frame. The crazy thing was that the circumference points and lines passed over the cleft, as if it had been of no importance to the creator of the pattern.

Extending on the form's left-hand side, the base line of the great square became the centre of a double circle. The same thing was repeated on the right-hand side, where there were two more large rings, one lying inside the other. From the centre ran straight lines in the four directions of the compass. From a great height the three diagrams presented a phenomenal picture: in the foreground the giant main circle framed by the two squares, then right and left the two connected rings. And everything connected by lines to everything else. If a thick stroke were to be drawn over the whole thing, the image of a gigantic arrow would emerge. . . .

Discovering a Pattern

Suddenly I cried out: 'Stop!', realizing at the same time how impossible my order was—we were after all in an aeroplane. I had glimpsed something, though only for a fraction of a second.

'What was it?' asked Eduardo.

'No idea,' I shouted back. But it was something. I saw strange points glinting. Let's go back.'

Eduardo flew round while I strained my eyes to see what was below. Because of the missing door I had a better view than my pilot. After circling again I was very disappointed— I had seen nothing more, yet was absolutely certain that there was something unusual below. At the third flight round, this time at 500 metres, I began to exclaim with joy.

'Look, Eduardo, look! Unbelievable! Here, right below me!'

Eduardo tipped the plane to one side. Then he saw it too.

On the summit of a mountain lay a chessboard of white points and lines—another phenomenal discovery. It was a giant, rectangular design, also with a cleft running through it. To its left ran some narrow 'Nazca lines' in pairs. This 'chessboard' consisted of 36 lines across and 15 lengthways, arranged in dots and dashes like Morse code. The whole pattern lay on an uneven summit. To its right was a steep slope, and below in the valley a dried-up river bed. . . .

Landing Aids

Here we have, then—for all who care to see—nothing other than geometry and mathematics. But for what purpose? One thing I realized straightaway was that both the chessboard and the gigantic geometrical form were visible only to those who knew how to fly. A non-flyer would have no chance of seeing these two patterns. Even if someone came across them by chance in the course of a crazy hike across the mountains in baking heat, he wouldn't be aware of them. But anyway, no path leads to them, and no mountain gods, however magic and mystical, would be of much use in getting there. No, these patterns were made for flyers. . . .

A Theory of Nazca

The Sanskrit literature of ancient India described how there were once gigantic space cities which orbited the earth. To check this, I suggest that my critics look up the 'Drona Parva' volume of the *Mahabharata*. (Every fair-sized university library should have a copy of this work.) It was translated into English in 1888 by the then renowned Sanskrit scholar Professor Protap Chandra Roy. At that time, Professor Chandra Roy could not have dreamt that such things as 'space-towns' might one day actually exist. Page 690, verse 62 of the 'Drona Parva' reads: 'Originally the brave Asuras possessed three towns in the heavens. Each of these towns was great and excellently built. . . . In spite of all his weaponry, Maghavat did not succeed in making any impression upon these heavenly towns. . . . ' And on page 691, verse 50 it states: 'then the three towns in the firmament met together. . . . ' It should be clear from this passage that some vague heaven of spiritual contentment is not meant, but rather the *firmament*, the physical heavens above us.

From these space-towns various types of aircraft, which the Indians called *vimanas*, visited the earth. One of these landed in the Nazca region. Of course it needed no *runway*, and anyway, no one would yet have made one. Why should a contingent of extraterrestrials land in the arid and inhospitable region of Nazca? Because the area is chock-full of minerals: iron, gold and silver. Drilling is still carried out there, and south-east of Nazca, intensive mining continues. The Marcona mine is the largest in Peru—not only for iron, but for minerals of all kinds.

Critics . . . who say that the ground under the surface of Nazca is too soft to bear the weight of a heavy machine understand nothing about space travel. The Americans no doubt worried about the same problem before the moon landing. No one knew whether the moon surface would support a spaceship as it landed—but a technological society can resolve such uncertainties.

The landing created a trapezoid surface on the ground. The trapezoid is broadest where the landing craft put down, and narrowest where the eddies of air made least impact on the ground.

From distant hills and mountains the native Indians watched the activities of the strangers with fear and astonishment. Human-like beings with golden, shimmering skins walked around, bored holes in the ground, gathered rocks and did unknown things with strange tools. Then one day there was a thunderous noise. The Indians rushed to their observation posts and saw the 'heavenly chariot' ascending into the sky.

That was the beginning of Nazca as a place of pilgrimage. It was now 'holy ground'. The gods had been there! . . .

A Place of Worship

Being inquisitive, as people are, small groups kept coming back to this mystical place. They talked together and assured one another that it had really happened, that chariots of the gods had come down from the heavens. But what did the signs that the gods had left behind them mean? Could they have meant that human beings should make similar designs for the gods? Was this what the heavenly powers expected of mankind? . . .

Years and decades passed, generations came and went. The priests observed the sky: from up there, from those distant points of light, the gods had once come. This was well known, for people now dead had seen it with their own eyes. But why did the gods not return? Had human beings somehow angered them, committed some fault that should be made good or repented? The toil in the desert was seen as a kind of 'sacrifice'. The more a person slaved away, the 'purer' he would seem in the eyes of the gods. The more impressive an earth marking appeared, the greater would be the gods' reward. This was also the reason why one tribe began to level the summit of one of the smaller mountains, and to scratch an ornamented runway out of the ground. It is a wonderful sight: the light strip on a darker background, with a kind of flower design emerging at its end. It was a particularly impressive invitation to the heavenly ones to land here rather than on a competitor's territory.

At some point people began to think they ought to tell the heavenly ones that they were expected and hoped for here on earth. The best way of doing this was to give a sign to heaven. Perhaps the chieftains also believed it was important to engrave their tribal symbols in a particularly lasting form into the ground, so that the heavenly ones would see them and bless their people. So the hard grind started all over again. Now the Indians carried stones away and began to scratch and scrape large areas. Ropes were laid out to guide this work. After the first tribal symbol had been completed— a spider—the artists among the Indians quickly noticed that the proportions were not right and that the curves were irregular. So they applied a simple method to improve the designs. With a wooden stick one of them etched a simple spider in the ground, no bigger than he could easily see at a glance. Then he laid small bright stones on his model, each stone representing a child. The children were called together and each one took up the position of one of the stones, though the children were spread out across the landscape on a much larger scale. They often had to be redirected because they weren't standing in the right place. But finally the wonder was achieved: a huge figure arose from a small model.

A Stunning Assessment

Whether it was like that or a little different we do not know. I am not even certain that the first, most ancient landing was by extraterrestrials. Perhaps a vimana just flew by carrying human passengers, as described in ancient literature. But one thing is crystal clear to me: someone made a landing at some time, and then several more later on, otherwise landing-approach systems would not have been needed. Over many centuries the region became a cult site. The facts, engraved into the earth, prove it. And the reality of the runway on the Cordillera de Chicauma in Chile, at a height of 2,400 metres, proves that runway-building dates back to the very distant past.

The cat's-cradle network of lines also proves that many generations laid down signs that were different from their forefathers', often over the top of previous markings. One community might direct lines towards certain stars, while the next concentrated its artistry on the point of sunset at the beginning of autumn. If one tribe was content to make a narrow line of 900 metres, the next might think it should be 'endless', and culminate at a summit to serve the mysterious gods as an orientation point. And once one line had been drawn, the priests might consider that this was not enough, for tradition said that the gods had descended in heavenly chariots—which would make *two* furrows in the ground.

There is, let me say it again, no single, unifying system to be found at Nazca. The line and runway network is neither calendar nor map, neither cultural atlas nor astronomy book—and, naturally, no space-port either. There is no overall order, since each tribe and generation scratched different conceptions into the desert. And did this all begin because of prehistoric flights of some kind?

The figures on the mountain slopes make this clear—beings emanating rays, figures which point to the heavens with one arm and to the earth with the other. And not only in Nazca but from Chile to the southern USA as well. The same is true of the gods painted on ceramics and woven in cloth, which can be found all the way to Arizona—where to this day the Hopi Indians depict the heavenly visitors in the form of puppets. And let us not forget the deformed skulls, whether they belonged to actual 'gods' or were copied from them. If all this is not proof, if people are willing to ignore the facts in front of them, then a science based on gathering and collating information has lost its senses.

The Crop Circles Are Not Hoaxes

Freddy Silva

Over the past twenty years, more than ten thousand crop circles—large geometric patterns of flattened grain—have appeared worldwide. While many are almost universally recognized as hoaxes, others provoke debate. Most skeptics argue that crop circles are the work of pranksters, but many believe that the crop circle phenomenon cannot be explained so easily.

In this excerpt from his book *Secrets in the Fields* (2002), artist and cereologist (crop circle researcher) Freddy Silva argues that many crop circles are not hoaxes. Citing firsthand accounts of strange lights and humming sounds followed by spontaneous crop circle formation, Silva claims that crop circles represent energy manifestation patterns created by unknown life forms. While he does not believe that crop circles are the direct work of alien spacecraft as such, he does believe that the circle makers are of extraterrestrial origin.

Freddy Silva, *Secrets in the Fields: The Science and Mysticism of Crop Circles*. Charlottesville, VA: Hampton Roads Publishing Company, Inc., 2002. Copyright © 2002 by Freddy Silva. Reproduced by permission of the publisher.

On the night of July 13, 1988, around 11:30 P.M., Mary Freeman was driving south next to the Avebury stone avenue. She noticed how the underside of a cloud near Silbury Hill had a golden white glow and was a great deal brighter than the glow from the Moon, which was not full. The hazy shape of an oval object seemed to protrude from inside the cloud. Suddenly, a tubular beam, as wide as a football field, plunged out of the cloud towards the ground to the south of Silbury. Freeman changed her direction of travel and raced towards the beam, which remained in place for some three minutes.

She remembered this incident clearly because all the objects in her car suddenly levitated around her as if the vehicle had been caught up in an energy field. Within thirty-six hours, farmer Roger Hues discovered the first of the five "Celtic Cross" formations at the base of Silbury Hill.

Three years later, a young man out riding his bike in Burleigh, Somerset, heard a high-pitched humming sound. As he looked up he saw a stationary, silver, bell-shaped craft project a spiraling vortex of "aura-like" light into a field and make a twenty-nine-foot crop circle in the early wheat, which in April was barely a foot high. The event was over in a few seconds and occurred in broad daylight (Wingfield 1991).

A similar experience occurred above the East Field, this time at midnight. Intrigued by a similar buzzing sound, a couple living nearby walked outside their house to find a set of colored lights swirling in the pitch-black sky. Twenty minutes later the lights congealed into one object from which a beam of white light descended onto the field. Five hours later the "DNA" crop glyph was discovered.

Given such clear incidences involving aerial phenomena popularly know as unidentified flying objects, we are faced

with postulating that an outside source is the agency responsible for interrupting the seasonal flow of cereal crops.
But, too, isn't it ridiculous to make "space brothers" the
likely culprits?

Enough material has been written on UFOs to stock a
generous-sized aircraft hangar, and I shall provide an
overview of this equally misunderstood area of knowledge.
If you are inclined to pursue it further, T.J. Constable's *The
Cosmic Pulse of Life* provides an excellent grounding in the
subject, as does Johannes von Buttlar's seminal work *The
UFO Phenomenon*, featuring scores of reliable and close-up
reports from civil and air force pilots. There are accounts of
daylight encounters, planes crashing, pilots killed in pursuit
of UFOs, and statements from air traffic controllers, states-
men, and even astronauts.

As with crop circles, human contact with UFOs predates
the twentieth century; in fact, it is recorded in the *Ramayana*,
one of the sacred Indian sagas, dating to 6000 B.C. Here you
will find written accounts of "two-storied celestial chariots
with many windows, roaring like lions and blazing with red
flames as they ascend into the sky to fly like comets"; the
Mahabharata and other Vedic and Sanskrit texts describe
similar events. In shamanic cultures throughout southern
Africa, UFOs are referred to as *abahambi abavutayo*, the "fiery
chariots" (Dutt 1961; Gordon 1962).

A papyrus stored in the Vatican tells of a UFO sighting in
Egypt during the reign of Tuthmosis III in 1500 B.C. The object is described as emitting a "foul odour," an observation often reported by latter-day victims of close encounters. In the
Chronicle of William of Newburgh, 1290, it is written that the
abbot of Byland Abbey in Yorkshire was about to say grace
when, "John, one of the brethren came in and said there was
a great portent outside. Then they all ran out and Lo! a large
round silver object, not dissimilar to a disc, flew slowly over

them and excited the greatest terror"; a similar report of the period exists in Matthew of Paris' *Historia Anglorum*. . . .

The Crop Circle Connection

Senior citizens, children, policemen, even military personnel have reported large structured craft six to thirty-six hours before the appearance of crop circles. Farmers around the Barbury Castle area have witnessed military jets and helicopters scramble to intercept balls of light or silent flying objects which then proceed to toy with their chasers, sometimes blinking out and re-appearing behind the craft giving chase. Busty Taylor has witnessed so many rotating objects with blinking lights that during his time as a driving instructor he's used these sightings as a reliable test of his students' alertness at the wheel. That these objects are not the lurid imagination of quirky British country-folk is confirmed by identical reports from around the world, including eyewitnesses from rural areas of Romania, Hungary, and Russia, countries where the words "crop" and "circle" had, up to that point, never been associated.

Former Yorkshire police sergeant Anthony Dodd has written extensively about the connection between the increase in UFO activity prior to crop circle activity. In 1991, members of his UFO organization investigated an incident on June 29 in Bristol, England, when dozens of witnesses called the police shortly before midnight to report a large red object crossing the night sky above the city. After it descended into nearby fields, a helicopter appeared and began to give chase. When the craft shot away at high speed, the helicopter returned to the field, combing it with its powerful searchlight. The next morning, residents discovered a large dumbbell pictogram at the site (Dodd 1991).

The presumed circle-making craft are not necessarily large. With the increase in the number of visitors to crop circle sites since the 1990s, the number of eyewitnesses reporting small silver-colored spheres has steadily grown, one of the best examples being Steven Alexander's daytime footage of the blinking sphere below Milk Hill, the event witnessed at close quarters on the ground by a farm laborer.

The objects appear capable of traveling at high speed; they are noiseless in flight, but emit a loud hum when hovering in position above a field. They vary in size from tennis to beach ball, and are capable of maneuvering at sharp angles with dexterity and as the British military has experienced over Alton Priors, they can toy with helicopters at will. They are most often seen at night between the hours of 11 P.M. and 3 A.M., as colored balls of either exceptional luminescence or translucence. . . .

Putting together all these reports of flying objects, a pattern begins to emerge, and a confusing one at that. Large structured craft; small, silver, and seemingly physical spheres; small, *luminous*, and seemingly physical spheres; balls of light that run the gamut of the visible color spectrum—how can they be all these things?

This following example provides a clue to the nature of these so-called UFOs. While investigating a series of crop circles in Cornwall, CCCS [Centre for Crop Circle Studies] chairman George Bishop took photographs which later revealed a green globe and a strange red object; other images were pockmarked with translucent white globes. Bishop was adamant that these "balls of light" had not been visible at the time the images were shot. It was believed that a defect in the film processing had taken place (later proved not to be the case), until identical light phenomena appeared in other visitors' photos, nine in all, some even shot at night.[1]

Hundreds of examples of light phenomena have since

1. personal communication with George Bishop

been captured on film, and not just inside crop circles, but in stone circles, too.[2] With the exception of people of psychic ability, the "balls of light" are never visible to the naked eye at the time the photos are taken, suggesting they are forms of energy at various stages of manifestation.

Science has established that the physical world is made up of atoms spinning at very high rates. In questioning the nature of the Universe, many physicists and metaphysicians have developed an understanding that different rates of spin govern different states of matter, even consciousness. As such, UFOs, balls of light, and other "paranormal" phenomena are inhabitants of a reality governed by rates of spin (some call it vibration) that differ from ours. Hence they are as real on their plane of existence as we are on ours. To illustrate this point, our visual cortex is capable of seeing a tree as long as the atoms that make up the tree vibrate at the same frequency as the human eye and its information processing mechanism. If the tree's atoms were to vibrate at a rate 2 Hz below the frequency of the eye, the tree would either "disappear" or the eye would register the tree as a "ghost."

When objects from other levels of reality alter their rate of spin they are observed as increasingly physical phenomena in our dimension. Additionally, as their frequency moves along the electromagnetic spectrum we see these objects in different colors, as author and UFO researcher John Keel observed [in his book *The Mothman Prophecies*]: "When the objects begin to move into our spatial and time coordinates, they gear down from higher frequencies, passing progressively from ultraviolet to bluish green. When they stabilize within our dimension, they radiate energy on all frequencies and become a glaring white" (Keel 1975).

2. Many incidences of otherwise invisible balls of light have been photographed during controlled experiments by the Santa Barbara–based researchers Ed and Kris Sherwood of Millennium Research.

Mysticism and Life Force Energy

This ability to transubstantiate matter would require, among other things, an understanding of the illusion of time, the function of gravity, knowledge of the proposed three speeds of light, and the spinning vortex action of molecules (Myers and Percy 1999), techniques attributed in the past to mortals such as Jesus Christ, the prophet Mohammed, and the Greek philosopher Apollonius of Tyana (Ash and Hewitt 1990; Yogananda 1996).

Studies into bioplasmic energy fields and orgone energy by such notables as Rudolf Steiner, Wilhelm Reich, and Semison and Valentina Kirlian clearly show that we are surrounded by a life-force energy which is interactive, yet seemingly invisible to the limited human range of vision. Mechanistic thought has brainwashed us into believing this energy source does not exist but, on occasion, the etheric world does show itself. An aura, several inches thick, was witnessed around the Tibetan Grand Lama by Dr. Alexander Cannon, a distinguished scientist and celebrated psychiatrist of his day (Hall 1937). This same aura is graphically represented by the halo framing the heads of Jesus Christ and the Christian saints.

That this force is associated with consciousness was hinted by the Nobel Prize–winning father of quantum theory, Max Planck: "There is no matter as such! All matter originates and exists only by virtue of a force. We must assume behind this force the existence of a conscious and intelligent Mind. This Mind is the matrix of all matter."

It appears that a number of sources contribute to the creation of crop circles. Given that these forms can react to the thoughts of people in their vicinity, these forms are either conscious, or at the very least, intelligently directed. Regardless, the increasing sighting and filming of "structured" craft, balls of light, even tubes of light that seem to originate from beyond Earth's atmosphere, all support the hypothesis that an aerial-borne outside agency is involved.

Even so, we can rule out crop circles as landings by alien craft. Classic UFO accounts, such as the Australian "UFO nests," are generally associated with squashed plants, indentations, electronic disruption, paralysis, burns, and harmful radioactivity. For example, in 1954, a number of people saw a craft flatten a field of corn in Mexico; that circular area yielded no further plant growth after the incident (Randles and Fuller 1990). A Uruguayan farmer witnessed a rotating, glowing orange ball flatten grass into a circle, scorching it in the process; this incident caused electrical failure and the subsequent death of his dog.

Given the ground evidence of crop circles, such reports suggest that circlemaking and landing UFOs are two separate phenomena, albeit sharing some attributes (electronic disruption, for example). Whatever your stance on UFOs, the cumulative evidence that someone not entirely of terrestrial origin is associated with a significant number of crop circle events is beyond doubt, even if less than 20 percent of crop circles are preceded by a UFO or other intelligently behaving light phenomena.

References

David Ash and Peter Hewitt, *Science of the Gods: Reconciling Mystery and Matter*. Bath, UK: Gateway, 1990.

Trevor James Constable, *The Cosmic Pulse of Life*. Sudbury, UK: Neville Spearman, 1977.

Anthony Dodd, "UFO Update," *The Journal of UFO Investigation*, no. 1, 1991.

Ramesh Dutt, *Ramayana and Mahabharata*. London: Dent, 1961.

Timothy Good, *Above Top Secret: The Worldwide UFO Cover-Up*. London: Sidgwick & Jackson, 1987.

Cyrus Gordon, *Before the Bible*. London: Collins, 1962.

Manly P. Hall, *Freemasonry of the Ancient Egyptians*. Los Angeles: The Philosophers' Press, 1937.

J. Allen Hynek and Jacques Vallée, *The Edge of Reality*. Chicago: Regency, 1975.

John Keel, *The Mothman Prophecies*. New York: Dutton, 1975.

David Myers and David Percy, *Two-Thirds: A History of Our Galaxy*. London: Aulis, 1999.

P.D. Ouspensky, *A New Model of the Universe*. London: Kegan Paul, 1931.

Lucy Pringle, *Crop Circles: The Greatest Mystery of Modern Times*. London: Thorsons, 1999.

Jenny Randles and Paul Fuller, *Crop Circles: A Mystery Solved*. London: Hale, 1990.

Reuters, "IBM Sells Air Force New Supercomputer to Identify UFOs," November 22, 2000.

Leonard Stringfield, "Inside Saucer Post 3-0 Blue," *CRIFO*, Cincinnati: November 4, 1957.

Jacques Vallée, *The Invisible College*. New York: Dutton, 1975.

Terry Wilson, *The Secret History of Crop Circles*. Paignton, UK: CCCS, 1998.

George Wingfield, *The UFO Report 1992*. London: Sidgwick & Jackson, 1991.

Paramahansa Yogananda, *Autobiography of a Yogi*. London: Rider, 1996.

Chapter 4

Fact or Fiction?

Evidence That UFO Landing Sites Do Not Exist

An Alien Spacecraft Did Not Crash in New Mexico in 1947

Robert L. Park

In 1947 a mysterious object fell from the sky and crashed near the city of Roswell, New Mexico. For fifty years, the U.S. government claimed that it was a weather balloon. Anecdotal accounts indicated otherwise. Decades later, some even claimed to see alien bodies amid the wreckage. Many UFO researchers still believe that a UFO crash and subsequent cover-up—an event referred to as the "Roswell Incident"—gave the U.S. military access to extraterrestrial technology.

In 1997 the U.S. Air Force finally admitted that the crashed object was not a weather balloon. They now claim that it was Project Mogul, a flying spy microphone designed to detect Soviet nuclear missile tests. Ufologists generally dismiss this as a second, desperate cover story scraped together to silence critics.

In this article adapted from his book *Voodoo Science*

(2000), University of Maryland physics professor and retired air force lieutenant Robert L. Park defends the Project
Mogul explanation. What he does not defend is the U.S. Air
Force's decision to mislead the American public by describing Project Mogul as a weather balloon. That decision, he
argues, has given credibility to the claims of ufologists.

The current fascination with aliens can be traced back to
the strange events that took place near Roswell, New Mexico,
in the summer of 1947. On June 14 of that year, William
Brazel, the foreman of the Foster Ranch, seventy-five miles
northwest of Roswell, spotted a large area of wreckage about
seven miles from the ranch house. The debris included neoprene strips, tape, metal foil, cardboard and sticks. Brazel
didn't bother to examine it closely at the time, but a few
weeks later he heard about reports of flying saucers and
wondered if what he had seen might be related. He went
back with his wife and gathered up some of the pieces. The
next day he drove to the little town of Corona, New Mexico,
to sell wool, and while he was there he "whispered kind a
confidential like" to the Lincoln County sheriff, George
Wilcox, that he might have found pieces of one of those "flying discs" people were talking about. The sheriff reported the
matter to the nearby army air base—the same base, in fact,
where I would be stationed seven years later (before my
time, though, the Air Corps was still part of the army, and
the base was known as Roswell Army Air Field).

The army sent an intelligence officer, Major Jesse Marcel,
to check out the report. Marcel thought the debris looked
like pieces of a weather balloon or a radar reflector; in any
event, all of it fit easily into the trunk of his car. There the incident might have ended—except for the garbled account

the public-information office at the base issued to the press the next day. The army, the press office noted, had "gained possession of a flying disc through the cooperation of a local rancher and the sheriff's office." The army quickly issued a correction describing the debris as a standard radar target, but it was too late. The Roswell incident had been launched. With the passage of years, the retraction of that original press release would come to look more and more like a cover-up.

By 1978, thirty years after Brazel spotted wreckage on his ranch, actual alien bodies had begun to show up in accounts of the "crash." Major Marcel's story about loading sticks, cardboard and metal foil into the trunk of his car had mutated into the saga of a major military operation, which allegedly recovered an entire alien spaceship and secretly transported it to Wright Patterson Air Force Base in Ohio. Even as the number of people who might recall the original events dwindled, incredible new details were added by second- and third-hand sources: There was not one crash but two or three. The aliens were small, with large heads and suction cups on their fingers. One alien survived for a time but was kept hidden by the government—and on and on.

A Real Cover-Up

Like a giant vacuum cleaner, the story had sucked in and mingled together snippets from reports of unrelated plane crashes and high-altitude parachute experiments involving anthropomorphic dummies, even though some of those events took place years later and miles away. And, with years' worth of imaginative energy to drive their basic beliefs, various UFO "investigators" managed to stitch those snippets into a full-scale myth of an encounter with extraterrestrials—an encounter that had been covered up by the government. The truth, according to the believers, was simply too frightening to share with the public.

Roswell became a gold mine. The unverified accounts spawned a string of profitable books, and were shamelessly exploited for their entertainment value on television programs and talk shows—even serious ones, such as CBS's *48 Hours* then hosted by the eminent anchorman Dan Rather, and CNN's *Larry King Live.* The low point was reached by Fox TV. In 1995 the network began showing grainy black-and-white footage of what was purported to be a government autopsy of one of the aliens—a broadcast that garnered such exceptional ratings (and such exceptional advertising revenues) that it was rerun repeatedly for three years. Then, when ratings finally began to wane, Fox dramatically "exposed" the entire thing as a hoax.

In 1994, to the astonishment of believers and skeptics alike, a search of military records for information about the Roswell incident uncovered a still-secret government program from the 1940s called Project Mogul. There really had been a cover-up, it turned out—but not of an alien spaceship.

Project Mogul

In the summer of 1947 the U.S.S.R. had not yet detonated its first atomic bomb, but it had become clear by then that it was only a matter of time. It was imperative that the United States know about the event when it happened. A variety of ways to detect that first Soviet nuclear test were being explored. Project Mogul was an attempt to "listen" for the explosion with low-frequency acoustic microphones flown to high altitudes in the upper atmosphere. The idea was not entirely harebrained: the interface between the troposphere and the stratosphere creates an acoustic channel through which sound waves can propagate around the globe. Acoustic sensors, radar tracking reflectors and other equipment were sent aloft on long trains of weather balloons, in the hope that they would be able to pick up the sound of an atomic explosion.

The balloon trains were launched from Alamogordo, New Mexico, about a hundred miles west of Roswell. One of the surviving scientists from Project Mogul, the physicist Charles B. Moore, professor emeritus at the New Mexico Institute of Mining and Technology in Socorro, recalls that Flight 4, launched on June 4, 1947, was tracked to within seventeen miles of the spot where Brazel found wreckage ten days later. Then, Moore says, contact was lost. The debris found on the Foster Ranch closely matched the materials used in the balloon trains. The Air Force now concludes that it was, beyond any reasonable doubt, the crash of Flight 4 that set off the bizarre series of events known as the Roswell incident. Had Project Mogul not been highly secret, unknown even to the military authorities in Roswell, the entire episode would probably have ended in July 1947.

It is hard to understand why Project Mogul was secret at all. Even before the Soviets tested their first atomic bomb, the project was abandoned, pushed aside by more promising detection technologies. There was nothing in Project Mogul that could have provided the Soviets with anything but amusement, yet it was a tightly kept secret for nearly half a century: even its code name was secret. The project would still be a secret if not for an investigation initiated in 1994 by Steven H. Schiff, a Republican congressman from New Mexico. Schiff insisted that an all-out search for records and witnesses was needed to reassure the public that there had been no government cover-up in Roswell.

Case Closed?

By 1997 the Air Force had collected every scrap of information dealing with the Roswell incident into a massive report, in hopes of bringing the story to an end. In fact, the enormous task of locating and sifting through old files and tracking down surviving witnesses had actually begun even before Schiff's call for full disclosure. Responding to requests from self-appointed UFO investigators acting under the Freedom of Information Act had become a heavy burden on the Air Force staff at the Pentagon, and they were eager to get ahead of the Roswell incident. The release of *The Roswell Report: Case Closed* drew one of the largest crowds on record for a Pentagon press conference.

Although the people involved insist that it was mere coincidence, the Air Force report was completed just in time for the fiftieth anniversary of Brazel's discovery of the Project Mogul wreckage. Thousands of UFO enthusiasts descended on Roswell, now a popular tourist destination, in July 1997 for a golden-anniversary celebration. They bought alien dolls and commemorative T-shirts, and snatched up every book they could find on UFOs and aliens. The only book that sold poorly was the Air Force report.

If there is any mystery still surrounding the Roswell incident, it is why uncovering Project Mogul in 1994 failed to put an end to the UFO myth. Several reasons seem plausible, and they are all related to the fact that the truth came out almost half a century too late. The disclosures about Project Mogul were pounced on by UFO believers as proof that everything the government had said before was a lie. What reason was there to think that Project Mogul was not just another one?

Furthermore, Project Mogul was not the only secret government program that bolstered belief in UFOs. During the cold war, U-2 spy planes often flew over the Soviet Union. At first, U-2s were silver-colored, and their shiny skins strongly reflected sunlight, making them highly visible—particularly in the morning and evening, when the surface below was dark. In fact, the CIA estimates that more than half of all the UFO reports from the late 1950s and throughout the 1960s were actually sightings of secret U-2 reconnaissance flights. To allay public concerns at the time, the Air Force concocted far-fetched explanations involving natural phenomena. Keeping secrets, as most people learn early in life, inevitably leads to telling lies.

Concealment and Public Trust

But secrecy, it seems, is an integral part of military culture, and it has generated a mountain of classified material. No one really knows the size of that mountain, and despite periodic efforts at reform, more classified documents exist today than there were at the height of the cold war. The government estimates that the direct cost of maintaining those records is about $3.4 billion per year, but the true cost—in loss of credibility for the government—is immeasurable. In a desperate attempt to bring the system under control, in 1995 President Clinton issued an executive order that will automatically declassify documents that are more than twenty-five years old—estimated at well in excess of a billion pages—beginning this year [2000].

Recent polls indicate that a growing number of people think the government is covering up information about UFOs. Nevertheless, it is easy to read too much significance into reports of widespread public belief in alien visits to earth. The late astronomer and science popularizer Carl Sagan saw in the myth of the space alien the modern equivalent of the demons that haunted medieval society, and for a susceptible few they are a frightening reality. But for most people, UFOs and aliens merely add a touch of excitement and mystery to uneventful lives. They also provide a handy way for people to thumb their noses at the government.

The real cost of the Roswell incident must be measured in terms of the erosion of trust. In the interests of security, people in every society must grant their governments a license to keep secrets, and in times of perceived national danger, that license is broadened. It is a perilous bargain. A curtain of official secrecy can conceal waste, corruption and foolishness, and information can be selectively leaked for political advantage. That is a convenient arrangement for government officials, but in the long run, as the Roswell episode teaches, it often backfires. Secrets and lies leave the government powerless to reassure its citizens in the face of far-fetched conspiracy theories. Concealment is the soil in which pseudoscience flourishes.

The Nazca Lines Are Not UFO Landing Aids

Anthony F. Aveni

The Nazca line drawings of southeastern Peru have inspired a great deal of speculation. As large geometric designs fully visible only from the air, carved over a millennium before the Wright Brothers invented the airplane, they might naturally lead one to wonder: Could extraterrestrials have built this?

In this excerpt from his book *Between the Lines: The Mystery of the Giant Ground Drawings of Ancient Nasca, Peru* (2000), Anthony F. Aveni criticizes theories that attribute the Nazca line drawings to extraterrestrial or supernatural forces. Aveni serves as Russell B. Colgate Professor of Astronomy and Anthropology at Colgate University, and has written twenty books on ancient civilization. He argues that the Nazca sculptors may well have had a self-contained artistic vision of their own.

117

Remember Atlantis? Ups and downs together with a distaste for and distrust of the official historical record formed the base of the Atlantis theory: civilizations come and go on our planet, rising and falling like a ride on a historical roller coaster. In the past we raised ourselves to far loftier heights than we experience in the present. Such was the view toward Atlantis. Just look at Egypt, where art, architecture, and hieroglyphic writing appear unified and full blown, without a hint of development out of a single primitive state, not to mention the Maya, Aztec, and Greek myths all telling of repeated cataclysmic destructions of past worlds.

The real Atlantis (and there may have been many of them around the world) had all the trappings of modern civilization, including electricity and internal-combustion engines. Discontent arose, just as in the modern world, out of factional differences in an economic system run by unregulated big business interests. No wonder lost continents were popular in the days of [industrial tycoons John D.] Rockefeller and [J.P.] Morgan!

At least since the classical age, say Atlantists, we have been riding the downslope, the evil powers in our society destroying and suppressing past knowledge. History is rife with book burning, from ancient China to Greek Alexandria to the destruction of the Maya codices by Spanish conquistadores. Having fallen out of harmony with nature, we are headed for another Armageddon. Learn the lesson of Atlantis, so say the prophets and proponents.

"All the great examples of antiquity . . . served to locate man in the cosmos, both in space and time, bringing knowledge of the heavens to the earth."[1] The ziggurats of Babylon, Egypt's pyramids, Mexico's temples—the measures of each of them, their ratios and their square roots, encapsulated the diameter of the earth, the distance to the moon, the spacing of the planets from the sun, even the basic dimensions of the tiniest atoms. Universal constants like pi and the golden mean, fundamental time units like the length of the month, the year, and the 26,000-year period of the precession of the equinoxes, all the magic numbers that underlie the blueprint of our universe are secretly locked away in the spacings between pyramids. If all of this sounds like a protest emanating from the restless industrialized world of the late eighteenth and early nineteenth centuries—a society dissatisfied with the course of civilization that was led to search for enlightenment by looking backward—guess again. It was the 1960's, the dawning of the Age of Aquarius. This gaze toward the future was wrought from a different set of dissatisfactions; still, the eye had taken on that same decidedly backward cast toward a presumed repository of superior knowledge, and there were plenty of elaborately illustrated, convincing-looking coffee-table books to tempt the public by providing conduits to the fountain of lost knowledge. Ancient remains became the legacy of previous races that once possessed all the knowledge of modern physics, mathematics, and astronomy and were wise enough to encode it into their mammoth architecture for posterity—just for us. Peter Tompkins, who wrote the words that head this paragraph, is among a cadre of popular writers who believe in such lost knowledge.

Explaining the Nasca Lines

Where there are leaders there will always be followers. In the wake of Paul Kosok's and Maria Reiche's theories about the great scientific achievement of the Nasca timekeepers, coupled with Tompkins's secret knowledge texts, high-tech fantasizers befitting the age would come to the pampa. Arch diffusionist Maria Scholten d'Ebneth carried the directions and proportions she found in Nasca geometry all the way over the globe to the Andean highlands and beyond, as far as the land of the Maya. The patterns on the Nasca textiles prove that " anthropogeometry" lay at the basis of the Nasca figures, she said, for the proportions of both place the relative locations of Cuzco, Tiahuanaco, and Pachacamac at key points of the design. She even included a map of the Americas to prove it. The Internet has yielded up a wondrous array of Nasca hypotheses that probably tell us more about us than them. For example, there is the story about the group of black slaves who rebelled against Tiahuanaco. Originally Olmecs from Mexico, they stole Viracocha's aircraft (presumed to be a real person, Viracocha is dubbed the original architect of the Nasca lines), flew to Nasca, and became the first vandals on the pampa when they attempted to obliterate his aircraft runways.

The New Age also spawned ingenious high-tech explanations for the Nasca lines. "I know damned well someone flew at Nasca. You simply can't see anything from ground level. You can't appreciate any of it from anywhere but from above," wrote the adventurer Jim Woodman.[2] Remember the Nasca flying creature whose painted image adorns so many late polychrome pots? Could he be engaged in the very posture necessary to appreciate the Nasca lines? Might he even be supervising their construction? What convinced Woodman that the Nasca drawings were meant to be seen from the air was a short flight over the pampa in a Cessna in 1973. Like so many before him in this age of customized discovery, Woodman discovered the Nasca lines for himself. All it took for him to conjure up an explanation that suited his own perspective was a strong conviction that all people solve practical problems by developing technological solutions. One way to appreciate a seeming maze of lines that antedated the era of flight, he reasoned, would be to devise a way to float above them in a lighter-than-air craft. . . .

Just how did the ancient people of Nasca manage to construct such a device? They used lightweight, tightly woven fabrics, the kind we find in textiles used as body bags at Nasca grave sites, Woodman proposed. Using Thor Heyerdahl's Kon-Tiki method, Woodman set out to prove that if he could do it, then they must have done it too. *Condor One* became the first balloon equal to the task at hand. Woodman and his sponsors, the International Explorers Society of Miami, Florida, crafted it from indigenous materials. The gondola was made of reeds, the balloon's 80-foot-high walls were woven with 185-by-95 threads to the square inch, and it was all laced together by reed cordage.

Woodman was fascinated by what he called burn pits, circular "scorched areas" at the ends of some of the trapezoids. He thought they were remnants of huge fires whose ascending heat columns were once used to power the balloons. That was how Woodman would power his *Condor One*—by holding its 52-foot opening for over four hours above a conduit connected to a roaring fire.

Believe it or not! The expedition was ingenious and the experiment a total success. One would hardly think it possible to inflate 80,000 cubic feet of bag with a smoke fire and then lift a 360-pound load to a height of 400 feet over the pampa and hold it there for two full minutes. Woodman's feat awed even the imperturbable Maria Reiche, who made a rare public appearance for the flight, as the desert aviator triumphantly concluded, "Nasca was not an ancient landing field, it was just the opposite. The lines were takeoff sites for a religion that worshipped the sun. My flight was a modern demonstration of an ancient religious ceremony."[3] . . .

Alien Landing Sites?

Of all that has been written about the pampa, there is one author above all others who eclipses even the revered Santa

Maria [Reiche] when it comes to popular recognition. It may come as a surprise that this particular individual spent no more than a few days on the pampa, yet his ideas still resonate throughout pop culture. Erich von Daniken is the archetype of the con man in an age of gullibility, especially when it comes to the interpretation of antiquity. What I find so ingenious about the way the Swiss hotelier turned antiquarian decoder captured the public's fancy is that he offered them an ideal contemporary parallel to the lost-world theories of the nineteenth and early twentieth centuries. What is different is that he seeks the source of higher knowledge in superior aliens far away in space rather than advanced terrestrial civilizations far backward in time—the ancient mysteries monomyth with a clever space-age twist. In his 1968 bestseller, *Chariots of the Gods*, he basically tells us that if it *looks* like an airfield, then it *was* an airfield.[4] Space aliens gave rise to our culture by interbreeding with earthlings. At Nasca they laid out runways on which to taxi in, land, and take off. The natives copied them. They made the lines to induce the extraterrestrials to return, the way the Papuans after World War II created metal birds out of old aircraft parts, cleared and leveled the jungle, and lit it up brightly at night to entice the visitors (American pilots) to come down from the sky, those gods in their flying machines.

Where do the animal geoglyphs fit into Daniken's astronaut scenario? When the gods from space failed to return, the people created the zoomorphs as sacrificial symbols. As proof of the runway hypothesis, Daniken displays a photograph of a turn bay on one of the alien aircraft runways. It turns out to be a 2-yard-wide segment of the condor's legbone.

Defenders of the extraterrestrial hypothesis cite plenty of evidence in literature from around the world to infer that we have been visited by aliens. Ezekiel's vision of the cherubim has been likened by many another writer to the first recorded appearance of a UFO:

> As I looked, behold, a stormy sign came out of the north, and a great cloud, with brightness round about it, and fire flashing forth continually, and in the midst of the fire, as it were gleaming bronze. And from the midst of it came the likeness of four living creatures. And this was their appearance: they had the form of men, but each had four faces, and each of them had four wings. Their legs were straight, and the soles of their feet were like the sole of a calf's foot; and they sparkled like burnished bronze. Under their wings on their four sides they had human hands. . . . Their appearances was like the gleaming of chrysolite; and the four had the same likeness, their construction being as it were a wheel within a wheel. When they went, they went in any of their four directions without turning as they went. The four wheels had rims and they had spokes; and their rims were full of eyes round about. And when the living creatures went, the wheels went beside them; and when the living creatures rose from the earth, the wheels rose. Wherever the spirit would go, they went, and the wheels rose along.[5]

Daniken cites it too. For him a vision is a vision and the ancient scriptures literally say what they mean.

Archaeologist William Stiebing Jr. thinks Daniken may have pulled heavily on the immensely popular science-fiction film *2001: A Space Odyssey*, which also appeared in 1968.[6] It included technologically advanced aliens whose legacy is confronted by our apelike ancestors. Daniken also took a lead from the then-popular (and recently revived) theory of panspermia, the idea that all humanity arose from life-giving spores that drifted through space and landed on earth millions of years ago.

Without a doubt, Daniken hardened the views of the French adventurer Robert Charroux.[7] He saw the whole pampa as a monumental exercise in the collective unconscious directed upward and far away toward our "Initiators," adding with a twinge of mysticism: "It is logical to assume that those Pre-Incas either were in contact with the Initiators mentioned by tradition or had preserved a memory of them. Thousands of years ago, in obedience to direct orders from the Initiators or for the purpose of perpetuating the teachings they had received in the past, they . . . created the vast page of writing that is Nasca."[8] Because the planet Venus is the companion of the sun god Inti in Andean lore, Charroux deduces that the extraterrestrials are none other than veritable Venusians, and because all great ideas offer an explanation for just about everything, he adds, "On this hypothesis, the drawings of birds at Nasca represented the spacecraft of the gods; the spirals, lines and geometric figures represented their landing installations; the flowers represented an offering; and the animals represented the ritual blood sacrifice that primitive people have always felt they owed to the gods: A form of worship, but also an appeal to the ancient visitors, an invitation for them to return."[9] Like Daniken, Charroux has an explanation for just about every mystery on the face of the earth, from the Turkish Piri Réis map to the Egyptian pyramids. All are products of the great beyond.

What should we make of such grandiose ideas that would have us reach out to other galaxies in search of answers to the Nasca mystery? Historian Jacquetta Hawkes once wrote of Britain's great enigma, "Every age has the Stonehenge it desires—or deserves."[10] She was critical of high-tech scientists, rushing headlong into one of Britain's most ancient monuments, computers in tow, to decode the mystery of Stonehenge without even looking at the archaeological or other cultural evidence. Likewise, in an age of technological achievement and dependence, the public fascination with the more splendid artifacts of ancient man has teased out some rather narrow-minded, present-centered explanations for the Nasca lines. As Daniken put it, "Incredible technical achievements existed in the past. There is a mass of know-how which we have only partially re-discovered today."[11] Like many other popularizers, Daniken assumes that all that lies between us and them is knowledge quite like our own. It has only become lost in time. In the end, I think this direct-pipeline approach to the past is too facile, too superficial, too ego- and ethnocentric to help us understand the meaning of the Nasca lines, for it relies solely on the sphere of experience of the modern world. . . . What compels us to deny the possibility that other civilizations can create ideas we ourselves had never contemplated? Are we so narcissistic that we can admire no motives for collective human action other than the ones that drive us?

Notes

1. P. Tompkins, *Mysteries of the Mexican Pyramids* (New York: Harper, 1976), p. 304. Other influential works by Peter Tompkins include *Secrets of the Great Pyramid* and *The Secret Life of Plants.*

2. J. Woodman, *Nazca Journey to the Sun* (New York: Simon and Schuster/Pocket Books, 1977), p. 39.

3. Ibid., p. 201

4. E. von Daniken, *Chariots of the Gods* (New York: Bantam, 1968).

5. Ezekiel 1: 4–8, 16–21.

6. W. Stiebing Jr., *Ancient Astronauts, Cosmic Collisions, and Other Popular Theories About Man's Past* (Buffalo, NY: Prometheus, 1984).

7. R. Charroux, *The Mysteries of the Andes* (New York: Avon, 1974). Evan Hadingham has traced the idea of "beacons for the gods" back even further, to works of the mid-fifties, when a few authors threatened to sue Daniken for plagiarism (*Lines to the Mountain Gods*, p. 54).

8. Charroux, *Mysteries of the Andes*, p. 173.

9. Ibid., pp. 179–80.

10. J. Hawkes, "God in the Machine," *Antiquity* 41 (1967): pp. 174–80.

11. Daniken, *Chariots of the Gods*, p. vii.

The Crop Circles Are Hoaxes

Joe Nickell

In the late 1970s, cheerful pranksters Doug Bower and Dave Chorley read a newspaper article about "crop circles"—geometric patterns of flattened grain crops—that had appeared in Queensland, Australia, and the subsequent panic about purported UFO landings. Looking for something fun to do on Friday nights, they decided to try the same trick in their native southern England—and it worked. Many of their crop circle designs attracted huge crowds of visitors and were attributed to unstable ion vortices or extraterrestrials. On September 8, 1991, they admitted the ruse and showed British newspapers how they had designed their crop circles. They were not, of course, the only source of crop circles in England (the number of crop circles produced annually has actually increased since they went public), but they were among the earliest, and they illustrated just how powerful well-crafted hoaxes could be.

In this article, Joe Nickell, a researcher for the Committee

Joe Nickell, "Circular Reasoning: The 'Mystery' of Crop Circles and Their 'Orbs' of Light," *Skeptical Inquirer*, vol. 26, September/October 2002, p. 17. Copyright © 2002 by the Committee for the Scientific Investigation of Claims of the Paranormal. Reproduced by permission.

for the Scientific Investigation of Claims of the Paranormal (CSICOP), argues that the crop circle phenomenon is driven by human beings very much like Doug Bower and Dave Chorley and not by extraterrestrials or other unexplained factors.

Since they began to capture media attention in the mid-1970s, and to proliferate and evolve through the decades of the 1980s and 1990s, crop circles have provided mystery and controversy. New books, touting "scientific research," continue the trend. The topic is also getting a boost from a new Hollywood movie, *Signs*, starring Mel Gibson as a Pennsylvania farmer who discovers a 500-foot design imprinted in his crops and seeks to learn its meaning.

At issue are swirled, often circular designs pressed into crop fields, especially those of southern England. They can range from small circles only a few feet in diameter to elaborate "pictograms," some now as large as a few hundred feet across. By the end of the 1980s books on the crop circle phenomenon had begun to spring up as well, and soon circles-mystery enthusiasts were being dubbed cereologists (after Ceres, the Roman goddess of vegetation). Circlemania was in full bloom.

Most cereologists—a.k.a. "croppies"—believed the circular designs were being produced either by extraterrestrials or by hypothesized "plasma vortices," supposedly "small, local whirlwinds of ionized air" (Haselhoff). A few took a more mystical approach. When I visited the vast wheat crops of the picturesque Wiltshire countryside in 1994, at one formation a local dowser told me he believed the swirled patterns were produced by spirits of the earth.

Hoaxers, most croppies insisted, could not be responsible

because the plants were only bent and not broken, and there were no footprints or other traces of human activity. Skeptics replied that from mid-May to early August the English wheat was green and pliable, and could only be broken with difficulty. As to the absence of tracks, they were precluded by de facto footpaths in the form of the tractor "tramlines" that mark the fields in closely spaced, parallel rows.

Investigation into the circles mystery indicated that it might be profitable to look not just at individual formations but at the overall phenomenon (rather on the old principle that one may fail to see the forest for the trees).

Four Suspicious Characteristics

Forensic analyst John F. Fischer and I soon identified several characteristics that suggested the work of hoaxers:

1. *An Escalation in Frequency.* Although there were sporadic reports of simple circles in earlier times and in various countries (possibly as UFO-landing-spot hoaxes), the classic crop circles began to be reported by the mid-1970s. Data on the circles showed that their number increased annually from 1981 to 1987, an escalation that seemed to correlate with media coverage of the phenomenon. In fact it appeared that the coverage helped prompt further hoaxes.

2. *Geographic Distribution.* The phenomenon showed a decided predilection for a limited geographic area, flourishing in southern England—in Hampshire, Wiltshire, and nearby counties. It was there that the circles effect captured the world's attention. And, just as the number of circles increased, so their locations spread. After newspaper and television reports on the phenomenon began to increase in the latter 1980s, the formations began to crop up (so to speak) in significant numbers around the world. Indeed the circles effect appeared to be a media-borne virus.

3. *Increase in Complexity.* A very important characteristic

of the patterned-crops phenomenon was the tendency of the configurations to become increasingly elaborate over time. They progressed from simple swirled circles to circles with rings and satellites, to still more complex patterns. In 1987 came a crop message, "WEARENOTALONE" (although skeptics observed that, if the source were indeed English-speaking extraterrestrials, the message should have read "You" rather than "We"). In 1990 came still more complex patterns, dubbed "pictograms." There were also free-form shapes (e.g., a "tadpole"-like design), a witty crop triangle, and the hilarious bicycle.

There also appeared beautifully interlinked spirals, a Menorah, intricate "snowflake" and stylized "spider web" designs, elaborate "Torus Knot" and "Mandala" emblems, pentagram and floral patterns, and other distinctive formations, including an "Origami Hexagram" and several fractals (mathematical designs with a motif subjected to repeated subdivision)—all consistent with the intelligence of modern *homo sapiens*. At the end of the decade came many designs that included decidedly square and rectilinear shapes, seeming to represent a wry response to the hypothesized swirling "vortex" mechanism.

4. *The Shyness Factor*. A fourth characteristic of the crop-field phenomenon is its avoidance of being observed in action. It is largely nocturnal, and the designs even appear to specifically resist being seen, as shown by Operation White Crow. That was an eight-night vigil maintained by about sixty cereologists in June 1989. Not only did no circles appear in the field chosen for surveillance but—although there had already been almost a hundred formations that summer, with yet another 170 or so to occur—not a single circle was reported during the period anywhere in England. Then a large circle-and-ring formation was discovered about 500 yards away on the very next day!

These and other characteristics are entirely consistent with the work of hoaxers.

The Hoax Factor

Indeed, as John Fischer and I were about to go to press with our investigative report, in September 1991 two "jovial con men in their sixties" confessed they had been responsible for many of the crop formations made over the years. In support of their claim the men, Doug Bower and Dave Chorley, fooled cereologist Pat Delgado. He declared a pattern they had produced for a tabloid to be authentic, insisting it was of a type no hoaxer could have made. The pair utilized a rope-and-plank device to flatten the plants, demonstrating their technique for television crews, e.g., on ABC-TV's "Good Morning America" on September 10, 1991.

Cereologists were forced to concede that hoaxers were producing elaborate designs and that "there are many ways to make a hoaxed crop circle" (Haselhoff). (For example, some who go 'round in circles use a garden roller to flatten the plants.) While in the past some cereologists thought they could distinguish "real" from fake circles by dowsing, the more cautious now admit it is not an easy matter, "certainly not as long as we do not even know exactly what mechanism creates crop circles" (Haselhoff). . . .

"Hovering Balls of Light"

Nevertheless, many circles aficionados have begun to photograph supposed [energy] vortex effects [at crop circle sites] which, curiously, resemble some of the same photographic anomalies that are the stock-in-trade of ghost hunters. For example, in her *Mysterious Lights and Crop Circles*, credulous journalist Linda Moulton Howe exhibits a flash photo taken in a crop circle that shows a bright "mysterious arch with internal structure that seems to spiral like a plasma."

Unfortunately for Howe (erstwhile promoter of cattle mutilations and similar "mysteries"), the effect is indistinguishable from that caused by the camera's unsecured wrist strap reflecting the flash. As corroborative evidence of this mundane cause, the bright strand-like shapes typically go unseen by the ghosthunter or cereologist, only appearing in their snapshots.

Again, Howe shows several photos containing "transparent spheres" that the croppies call "energy balls," "light orbs," "atmospheric plasmas," etc. They are indistinguishable from "orbs" of "spirit energy" typically seen in photographs of graveyards and other "haunted" places and that sometimes appear in snapshots as UFOs. Skeptics have demonstrated that these globelike effects can be produced by particles of dust, water droplets, and the like reflecting the flash. Other simulators of paranormal "energy" in photos include lens flares (the result of inter-reflection between lens surfaces), bugs and debris reflecting the flash, and many other causes, including film defects and hoaxes.

Sometimes, however, "hovering balls of light" and other "energy" effects are reported by eyewitnesses, though not only in the vicinity of crop circles. These too may have a variety of causes, including pranksters' parachute flares, various misperceived aerial craft and other phenomena (such as ball lightning), false claims, hallucinations, etc. In some instances, small lights observed moving about cropfields at night might have come from the flashlights of the circle makers!

It appears that for the foreseeable future the crop-circle phenomenon will continue. At least it has moved from the level of mere hoaxing—"a form of graffiti on the blank wall of southern England" (Johnson)—to represent an impressive genre of outdoor art. The often breathtaking designs (best seen in aerial photographs, like the giant Nazca drawings in Peru) are appreciated not only by the mystery mongers but by skeptics as well. Indeed as reliably reported [by Hoggart and Hutchinson], skeptics have helped to make many of them!

Notes

Burton, Garry. 1999. Welcome to 'Orb World.' http://members. aol.com/Analogsys/index 2.html.

Delgado, Pat, and Colin Andrews. 1989. *Circular Evidence.* Grand Rapids, MI: Phanes Press.

"Flares Spark Reports of UFOs." 1999. *Cornish Guardian,* August 19 (quoted in Howe 2000, 166–167).

Haselhoff, Eltjo H. 2001. *The Deepening Complexity of Crop Circles.* Berkeley, California: Frog, Ltd.

Hoggart, Simon, and Mike Hutchinson. 1995. *Bizarre Beliefs.* London: Richard Cohen Books, 52–61.

Howe, Linda Moulton. 2000. *Mysterious Lights and Crop Circles.* New Orleans, LA: Paper Chase Press.

Johnson, Jerold R. 1991. "Pretty Pictures," *MUFON UFO Journal,* 275: 18, March.

Mosbleck, Gerald. 1988. "The Elusive Photographic Evidence," in Spencer and Evans 1988, 210.

Nickell, Joe. 1994. *Camera Clues: A Handbook for Photographic Investigation.* Lexington: University Press of Kentucky.

———. 1995. "Crop Circle Mania Wanes. *Skeptical Inquirer* 19:3 (May/June), 41–43.

———. 1996a. "Levengood's Crop-Circle Plant Research. *Skeptical Brief* 6:2 (June), 1–2.

———. 1996b. "Ghostly Photos." *Skeptical Inquirer* 20:4 (July/August), 13–14.

Nickell, Joe, and John F. Fischer. 1992. "The Crop-Circle Phenomenon: An Investigative Report." *Skeptical Inquirer* 16:2 (Winter), 136–49.

Schnabel, Jim. 1994. *Round in Circles.* Amherst, NY: Prometheus Books.

Spencer, John, and Hilary Evans, eds. 1988. *Phenomenon: Forty Years of Flying Saucers.* New York: Avon.

Epilogue: Analyzing the Evidence

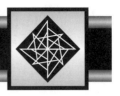

What a person believes about mysterious places can say a great deal about his or her worldview and understanding of life. Someone with a predominantly scientific approach to the universe will be more likely to see the Great Pyramid as an elaborate burial site and Stonehenge as an astronomical tool. Meanwhile, someone whose belief system is strongly oriented in spirituality may place more emphasis on their status as ancient sacred sites and may expect to see tangible signs of their rich spiritual legacy. Some sites—such as the Corona crash site near Roswell, New Mexico, and the great Nazca lines of Peru—inspire theories about extraterrestrial life, which in turn provoke countertheories from skeptics.

The readings in this book present specific theories about the origins of six mysterious sites. In this epilogue we will provide you with tools to evaluate the arguments and the evidence that authors often use to back up their theories.

About the Author

One of the first things you will notice about an argument is its author. Although an author's credentials and biases do not determine the quality of an argument, they can be used to estimate how credible and well-researched an author's data is likely to be. Has the author any special qualifications for writing about the subject? Is the author a respected writer known for accurate research? Does the author have any noticeable biases? The answers to these questions can give you a preliminary idea of what sort of argument you might encounter.

The Five-Step Approach

When an author presents an argument, he or she is essentially making a case; when you respond to that argument, you are essentially rendering a verdict. In a courtroom, juries are asked to consider the claim and the evidence, then reach a verdict based on the merits of the case. This process—also used by scientists and many philosophers—is called hypothetical reasoning. Although the term is used by different people in different ways, it has a common five-step process:

1. State the author's hypothesis (claim).
2. Gather the author's supporting evidence.
3. Examine the author's supporting evidence.
4. Consider alternative hypotheses (claims).
5. Draw your own conclusion about the author's argument.

If this sounds too easy, remember that hypothetical reasoning is a way of evaluating specific claims, not a shortcut to certainty. You are always welcome to suspend judgment on issues covered in this book if you have not made up your mind about them.

In the sections below, we will use hypothetical reasoning to evaluate two articles from this book. You can practice applying the method to as many of the other articles as you like.

Step 1: State the Author's Hypothesis

A hypothesis is a testable statement. For example, if you leave an ice cube on a table and return an hour later to find a small puddle in its place, you might hypothesize that the ice cube melted. Someone else might hypothesize that the ice cube was taken off the table by someone with wet hands. Most articles in this book make one or more claims about the world's mysterious places. Each article's title describes its main point. The following table shows some of the articles' main points restated as hypotheses:

Author	Hypothesis
Art Bell and Brad Steiger	(No central provable/disprovable hypothesis.)
Christopher Castle	(No central provable/disprovable hypothesis.)
Graham Hancock	The *moai* statues of Easter Island may have been built by an ancient globe-spanning civilization.
Evan Hadingham	
James Trefil	Stonehenge was built to serve as an astronomical calendar.
Jared Diamond	
Kevin D. Randle	In 1947 an alien spacecraft crashed near Roswell, New Mexico.
Erich von Däniken	The mysterious Nazca plain carvings in Peru are alien landing sites.
Freddy Silva	
Robert L. Park	
Anthony F. Aveni	The mysterious Nazca plain carvings in Peru are works of art carved by the ancient Peruvians.
Joe Nickell	Crop circles are the work of human beings.

A good hypothesis is always clear, specific, and either provable or disprovable:

1. *Clear.* The meaning of the hypothesis should be relatively obvious and stated in a concise way.

2. *Specific.* The hypothesis should be a specific claim, not a general one. For example, "There is more going on at the air force than meets the eye" is a fairly useless hypothesis. "The air force is hiding secrets about alien spacecraft" is more tangible. In cases where the argument itself is necessarily vague—for example, if the author is arguing that the air force is engaging in a massive cover-up but has no idea why—then the vagueness itself should be mentioned as part of the hypothesis ("The air force is engaging in a massive cover-up for unknown reasons").

3. *Provable (or disprovable).* It should be possible, at least in theory, to prove or disprove any hypothesis based on evidence. A hypothesis should state alleged fact, not pure opinion (though it can state an alleged fact *about* pure opinion, such as "Most Americans do not believe that extraterrestrials built the Great Pyramid"). The first two articles in the table above make clear statements about the authors' personal experiences with the sites in question (arguing, in effect, that there is more to these sites than meets the eye), but they do not translate those experiences into a single hypothesis that can be proven.

Four other articles in the table above do not have hypotheses listed. After reading the articles, try to translate each article's most important argument into a clear, specific, and provable hypothesis.

Kevin D. Randle: "An Alien Spacecraft Crashed in New Mexico in 1947"

Now that we have looked at the authors' hypotheses, let us apply the hypothetical reasoning process to one of them. Here we will discuss Kevin D. Randle's article, beginning on page 78.

Step 2: Gather the Author's Supporting Evidence

After determining what the author's claim is, we can take a look at how he or she intends to support it. For our purposes, *evidence* includes any idea or fact that the author uses to prove a claim. Here are ten pieces of evidence that Randle uses to support his hypothesis that an alien spacecraft crashed near Roswell, New Mexico, in 1947:

1. The July 8, 1947, issue of the *Roswell Daily Record* quotes U.S. Air Force officers as saying that they had "captured" a crashed flying saucer.

2. In 1978 one of the air force officers who had studied the flying saucer wreckage—Jesse Marcel—came forward and argued that what he had examined did not resemble a balloon and was "not something that was built on Earth."

3. Mack Brazel, the farmer who first discovered the Roswell wreckage, once stated in an interview, "I am sure what I found was not any weather observation balloon."

4. According to Brazel's son Bill (who claimed to have seen some of the crash debris), pieces of wreckage found at the Corona site exhibited unusual properties.

5. According to retired U.S. Air Force major Edwin Easley, Mack Brazel was kept under guard on an air force base after discovering the wreckage.

6. According to a co-owner of the radio station KGFL, the Federal Communications Commission and several state politicians threated to revoke the station's license if it broadcast an early interview with Mack Brazel.

7. According to "a half dozen of his friends," Brazel's second KGFL interview—in which he amended his story and stated that he had, in fact, found a weather balloon—was conducted under military escort.

8. According to his son, Mack Brazel was kept in military custody for six days after discovering the wreckage.
9. On July 10, 1947, photographs of the Project Mogul launch (the U.S. Air Force's explanation for the secrecy surrounding the Roswell incident) were published in "newspapers around the country."
10. The author believes that Project Mogul was not important enough to the military to justify the level of secrecy associated with the Roswell incident.

Step 3: Examine the Author's Supporting Evidence

As you can see, Randle makes a detailed and complex case for his hypothesis based on a great deal of diverse evidence. Here we will discuss three types of evidence used by Randle: eyewitness testimony, statements of fact, and opinions and expert testimonials.

Some evidence will inevitably fall into more than one category. This is not an uncommon occurrence and simply means that the evidence will need to be analyzed from multiple perspectives.

Eyewitness testimony (items 1, 2, 3, 4, 5, 6, 7, 8): Eyewitness testimony plays a significant role in human life, and its importance is difficult to overstate. We receive information on current events based on eyewitness testimony from journalists, and historians base much of their knowledge of the ancient world on recorded eyewitness testimony.

The drawback to eyewitness testimony is that it is the easiest kind of evidence to fabricate. Anyone can instantly generate a piece of eyewitness testimony by lying, and even honest eyewitnesses can be fooled, make an honest mistake, hallucinate, or remember incorrectly. Here are two factors worth considering when you find yourself presented with eyewitness testimony:

1. *The credibility of the witness.* Does the witness have a track record of dishonest or unreliable behavior? Alternately, does the witness have a track record of honest or reliable behavior? Does the witness stand to gain—or lose—anything by coming forward? What are the witness's relevant credentials? Was the witness intoxicated or under unusual personal stress at the time of the event (or testimony)? Could the witness be biased?

2. *The credibility of the testimony.* Can the testimony be corroborated by other eyewitness testimony or other forms of evidence? Alternately, is the testimony contradicted by other eyewitness testimony or other forms of evidence? Does it contradict itself? When the testimony is meant to describe a single specific event, was it recorded soon after the event—reducing the chances that the witness's memory has become hazy over time?

Some of Randle's evidence is eyewitness testimony. Much of it was gathered more than forty years after the original event, but many of the witnesses—who had served in the military, some of them in an exceptionally distinguished capacity—could be said to have an unusually honest track record, though some skeptics argue that Jesse Marcel had a reputation for hyperbole.

What do you think? After reading the article and considering the information provided in this section, do you find Randle's eyewitness testimony to be credible? What testimony do you find to be most credible?

Statements of fact (items 1, 9): A statement of fact is a direct claim that something is true. For example, "I saw a ghost in the hallway" is an example of eyewitness testimony, while "there was a ghost in the hallway" is a statement of fact. Statements of fact can be as complex and dubious as the claims they are used to support, or they can represent established principles and historical facts that can be easily verified using everyday reference materials. When you are confronted with a statement of fact that cannot be easily verified, it is usually helpful to mentally apply the same five-step hypothetical reasoning process to it that you would apply to larger arguments.

Randle's statement of fact is easy to verify but much more difficult to disprove. One could verify item 9 by finding any national or regional newspaper that published a photograph of the Project Mogul launch on July 10, 1947—but disproving it would require a comprehensive survey of every newspaper in the United States.

In your opinion, how useful is Randle's statement of fact?

Opinions and expert testimonials (items 1, 2, 3, 4, 10): Opinions tend to be among the weakest forms of evidence but can be convincing under certain circumstances. When an opinion is provided by an unbiased expert, it is referred to as an expert opinion, or testimonial. In a court of law, an expert witness—an unbiased individual who is particularly well versed in a given field—may be called upon to support or denounce a claim based on his or her credentials, experience, and reputation.

It is possible to weigh an opinion or testimonial using three steps:

1. *Determine the authority's credentials.* An opinion or testimonial is strongest when the source is better qualified to render an opinion on the subject than most of his or her audience. Most of us would accept whatever Stephen Hawking has to say about particle physics because he is regarded as an expert in the field, but we would be less likely to believe what a stand-up comedian has to say about the subject.

2. *Check for bias.* No matter what an expert's credentials may be, any hint of bias can call an opinion or testimonial into question. The president of a fast-food

chain may indeed know far more than most of us do about hamburgers, but we would be justifiably skeptical about any statements he or she made about the nutritional value of red meat.

3. *Whenever possible, double-check a quoted opinion or testimonial.* Sometimes, credible authority figures are (intentionally or unintentionally) quoted out of context to strengthen an argument. It is useful to know whether they really mean to say what they are quoted as saying.

In the case of item 10, the opinion is provided by the author himself. This means that he is not being misrepresented, but it is important to examine his biases. Randle has worked with UFO research groups and written many commercially successful books on the Roswell crash. These facts suggest that he has a propensity to believe in alien visitation in general and the Roswell crash in particular. On the other hand, his background in the U.S. Air Force adds some credibility to his judgments.

Step 4: Consider Alternative Hypotheses

The next step in examining a hypothesis is to see how it addresses alternative explanations for the evidence. Many authors fail to represent competing theories, or they represent them in an unfair and incomplete way. Although a one-sided argument is not necessarily a sign that the hypothesis is false, it is usually a sign that the author has not done a thorough job of supporting his or her claim.

The author's tone is sometimes a good indicator of how well he or she addresses alternative hypotheses. Does the author give the alternative hypotheses a reasonable amount of consideration and respect? If the author's tone seems patronizing or inappropriately hostile, he or she may not be considering the alternative hypotheses on a rational level.

Furthermore, an author who describes an alternative hypothesis in such a way that it seems obviously unbelievable is not giving fair consideration to competing arguments about a phenomenon.

Randle discusses the now-discredited weather balloon theory as well as the U.S. Air Force's more recent Project Mogul explanation. He gives much more attention to the former but does not appear to take either of them very seriously as explanations. He accepts the air force's rejection of the weather balloon theory and argues that Project Mogul is not a sufficient explanation for the secrecy over the events in Roswell because it was not a very well-kept secret in the first place.

In your opinion, does Randle do a thorough job of assessing alternative explanations for the Roswell incident?

Step 5: Draw Your Own Conclusion

After looking over the evidence and considering any other objections or concerns that you might have, you are in a position to evaluate the strength of the author's argument using hypothetical reasoning. Please note that this scale measures how much you agree with an author's argument, not how much you agree with the author's conclusion. Good arguments can be made on behalf of bad ideas, and vice versa. It is usually possible to classify your judgment of an author's argument into one of the following categories:

1. *Acceptance.* You find the author's argument to be extremely convincing. All of its major points are credible, and it has no substantial flaws.
2. *Limited acceptance.* The author's argument is compelling, but you have some reservations about it.
3. *Neutrality.* You do not feel ready to judge the author's argument. Perhaps it assumes knowledge in fields you are not familiar with or deals entirely with abstract ar-

guments that you do not feel qualified to evaluate.

4. *Limited disagreement.* The author's argument is fairly weak, but it contains enough merit to justify further discussion.

5. *Dismissal.* The author's argument completely falls apart under criticism. All important evidence is either unconvincing or misrepresented.

How would you rank Kevin D. Randle's argument? What are its strongest points? What are its weakest points? How would you improve it?

Joe Nickell: "The Crop Circles Are Hoaxes"

Let's apply hypothetical reasoning to another article, Joe Nickell's piece "The Crop Circles Are Hoaxes" on page 126.

Step 1: State the Author's Hypothesis

Crop circles are the work of human beings.

Step 2: Gather the Author's Supporting Evidence

1. Nickell believes that the spread of crop circles from England to other countries, which coincided with increased media coverage, suggests that the idea caught on and encouraged other human beings to create crop circles.

2. In response to an argument that man-made crop circles would feature broken plants rather than bent ones, Nickell argues that English wheat is flexible and easy to bend during the late spring and early summer months (when most crop circles are reported).

3. In response to an argument that man-made crop circles would show evidence of footprints, Nickell argues that any footprints would probably be covered up by tractor tracks.

4. In Operation White Crow (June 1989), sixty crop circle researchers kept an eye on English wheat fields for eight days in hopes of documenting the crop circle process. During that period, no crop circles were reported anywhere in England (despite the nearly three hundred English crop circles that would be reported that summer).

5. Nickell believes that the crop circles' increase in frequency, increase in complexity, and elusiveness are "entirely consistent with the work of hoaxers."

6. In September 1991 English hoaxers Doug Bower and Dave Chorley admitted that they had been making crop circles since the 1970s by flattening plants with a rope and plank.

7. Hoaxed crop circles can also be made using a garden roller.

8. Nickell sees some similarities between circle-making orbs of light photographed by crop circle researchers and orbs of light photographed by ghost hunters, and he believes that both categories of photographs can be attributed to photographic anomalies, natural phenomena, or hoaxers.

9. In Nickell's opinion, eyewitness accounts of light orbs can be explained by ball lightning, parachute flares, or other normal phenomena (including false claims, hallucinations, etc.).

Step 3: Examine the Author's Supporting Evidence

Joe Nickell's article argues that crop circles are created by human hoaxers. To support this claim, he uses much the same kinds of evidence that Kevin D. Randle uses—eyewitness testimony, statements of fact, and opinions and testimonials. He also uses generalizations and a scientific study.

Eyewitness testimony (item 2): Like most skeptical arguments, Nickell's article is essentially a response to eyewitness testimony; he uses very little of it himself, focusing on other types of evidence. In this case, he relies on personal experience in stating that English wheat can be easily bent during warm seasons.

Statements of fact (items 6, 7): Nickell makes two statements of fact about the spread of the crop circle phenomenon, information that would be fairly easy to verify.

Generalizations (items 6, 8): A generalization is a claim based on examples. For instance, an author might quote eyewitness testimony from three people who like grapefruit juice, then generalize that everyone does. Although this sort or argument is sometimes classified as a fallacy, it is a necessary part of everyday reasoning. We can believe that gravity always works, or that people walk on their feet rather than their hands, only by generalizing based on known cases. There are two types of generalizations:

1. *Explicit generalizations.* The author openly argues on behalf of the generalization.
2. *Implied generalizations.* The author presents evidence that would logically lead the audience to generalize. For example, an author might describe three famous cases of dog attacks, leaving many readers with the impression that dogs are dangerous.

Item 8 is an explicit generalization: Nickell clearly expresses a belief that the similarities between crop circle orb photographs and ghost photographs imply that they are caused by the same photographic anomalies. Item 6 is more implicit: In his discussion of the crop circle hoaxers Doug Bower and Dave Chorley, Nickell implies several times that most or all crop circles were also created as pranks. Some of Nickell's descriptions of crop circle research could also be described as implicit generalizations since he does not choose particularly flattering examples to represent the movement.

Opinions and expert testimonials (items 1, 2, 3, 5, 8, 9): Nickell, a longtime paranormal investigator with an impressive publication history, relies extensively on his background and professional judgment. On the other hand, he has two noticeable biases: He is the author of the piece, and he is a prominent and vocal member of the Committee for the Scientific Investigation of Claims of the Paranormal, a group for skeptics. This suggests that he is predisposed to disbelieve claims in support of paranormal or extraterrestrial phenomena.

Scientific studies (item 4): Authors will sometimes cite studies to support their conclusions. Scientific studies can be evaluated using a three-step process:

1. *Who conducted the study?* Was it supervised by a university or credible scholarly organization? Was it conducted by a biased or dishonest person or group?
2. *How was the study conducted?* Was it conducted in a fair and credible way? In the case of surveys, was the question worded in such a way that it might have encouraged a specific answer?
3. *When was the study conducted?* Does it rely on obsolete data or research methods? Has it been contradicted by more recent studies?

Nickell refers to Operation White Crow, a June 1989 vigil conducted by a group of crop circle researchers. He provides no citation information on the study, limiting our ability to evaluate it.

Step 4: Consider Alternative Hypotheses

Elsewhere in his article (in a section not included here), Nickell provides an extensive critique of an alternative theory of crop circle formation: the theory that the circles are created by an undiscovered natural phenomenon called plasma ion vortices. He does not, however, discuss other popular theories of crop circle formation in any substantial depth.

Step 5: Draw Your Own Conclusion

You decide: Does Joe Nickell make a good case that crop circles are the work of hoaxers? Where would you rank his argument on our five-point scale? How would you improve it?

Your Turn!

Choose one article from this book that has not already been analyzed and use hypothetical reasoning to decide whether the author's evidence supports the hypothesis. Here is a form you can use:

Name of article_____ Author_____

1. State the author's hypothesis.

2. Isolate the author's supporting evidence, listing each piece of evidence as part of a numbered list (as we did with the two articles analyzed above).

3. Examine the author's supporting evidence. Identify each type of evidence—is it eyewitness testimony, a statement of fact, an opinion or testimonial, a generalization, a scientific study, or something else entirely?

4. Consider alternative hypotheses. What alternative hypotheses does the author consider? Are they presented in a fair way? Can you think of any credible alternative hypotheses that the author might have missed?

5. Draw your own conclusion. Does the author make a convincing case?

For Further Research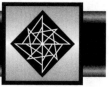

Anthony F. Aveni, *Ancient Astronomers*. New York: Smithsonian, 1995.

——, *Between the Lines: The Mystery of the Giant Ground Drawings of Ancient Nasca, Peru*. Austin: University of Texas Press, 2000.

——, *Stairways to the Stars: Skywatching in Three Great Ancient Cultures*. New York: Wiley, 1999.

Robert Bauval and Adrian Gilbert, *The Orion Mystery: Unlocking the Secrets of the Pyramids*. New York: Three Rivers/Crown, 1995.

Christopher Chippindale, *Stonehenge Complete*. Rev. ed. London: Thames & Hudson, 1994.

Erich von Däniken, *Arrival of the Gods: Revealing the Alien Landing Sites at Nazca*. Boston: Element, 1998.

——, *Chariots of the Gods? Unsolved Mysteries of the Past*. New York: Putnam, 1968.

——, *The Eyes of the Sphinx: The Newest Evidence of Extraterrestrial Contact in Ancient Egypt*. New York: Putnam, 1996.

——, *The Gods and Their Grand Design*. New York: Putnam, 1984.

——, *In Search of Ancient Gods: My Pictorial Evidence for the Impossible*. New York: Delacorte, 1976.

——, *Signs of the Gods*. New York: Putnam, 1980.

Paul Devereux, *Earth Mysteries*. London: Piatkus, 2000.

———, *Places of Power: Measuring the Secret Energy of Ancient Sites.* 2nd ed. London: Blanford, 1999.

Kendrick Frazier, Barry Karr, and Joe Nickell, eds., *The UFO Invasion: The Roswell Incident, Alien Abductions, and Government Coverups.* Amherst, NY: Prometheus Books, 1997.

Stanton T. Friedman and Don Berliner, *Crash at Corona: The U.S. Military Retrieval and Coverup of a UFO.* New York: Marlowe, 1992.

Evan Hadingham, *Circles and Standing Stones: An Illustrated Exploration of Megalith Mysteries of Early Britain.* New York: Walker, 1974.

———, *Early Man and the Cosmos.* Norman: University of Oklahoma Press, 1985.

———, *Lines to the Mountain Gods: Nazca and the Mysteries of Peru.* Norman: University of Oklahoma Press, 1988.

Graham Hancock and Robert Bauval, *The Message of the Sphinx: A Quest for the Hidden Legacy of Mankind.* New York: Three Rivers/Crown, 1997.

Graham Hancock and Santha Faiia, *Fingerprints of the Gods.* New York: Three Rivers/Crown, 1996.

———, *Heaven's Mirror: Quest for the Lost Civilization.* New York: Three Rivers/Crown, 1999.

———, *Underworld: The Mysterious Origins of Civilization.* New York: Three Rivers/Crown, 2002.

Zahi A. Hawass, *The Pyramids of Ancient Egypt.* New York: Carnegie Museum. 1990.

———, *Secrets from the Sand: My Search for Egypt's Ancient Past.* New York: Abrams, 2003.

Gerald Hawkins, *Stonehenge Decoded.* New York: Doubleday, 1965.

Thor Heyerdahl, *Easter Island: The Mystery Solved.* New York: Random House, 1989.

Kal A. Korff, *The Roswell UFO Crash: What They Don't Want You to Know.* New York: Dell, 2000.

J.P. Lepre, *The Egyptian Pyramids: A Comprehensive, Illustrated Reference.* Jefferson, NC: McFarland, 1990.

Catherine Orliac and Michel Orliac, *Easter Island: Mystery of the Stone Giants.* New York: Abrams, 1995.

Mike Pitts, *Hengeworld.* Rev. ed. New York: Random House, 2001.

Kevin D. Randle, *Case MJ-12: The True Story Behind the Government's UFO Conspiracies.* New York: HarperTorch, 2002.

———, *The Roswell Encyclopedia.* New York: Avon, 2000.

Freddy Silva, *Secrets in the Fields: The Science and Mysticism of Crop Circles.* Charlottesville, VA: Hampton Roads, 2002.

Jennifer Westwood, *The Atlas of Mysterious Places.* New York: Grove, 1987.

Richard Williams, *Earth's Mysterious Places.* New York: Reader's Digest, 1992.

Index

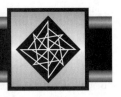